Packed full of fascinating facts, intertwined with inspirational thoughts, Then Sings My Soul *is a rich treasure and a riveting read.*

Catherine Campbell, author of *Rainbows for Rainy Days*

I simply love this book! Pam brings our precious old hymns back to life by telling us about the people who wrote them and why. Totally fascinating!

Jennifer Rees Larcombe, author

By the same author, published by Lion Hudson:

Non-fiction
Love So Amazing
Colours for the Soul
As Time Goes By
Love Bites

Fiction
With Hearts and Hymns and Voices
Fisher of Men (Dunbridge Chronicles 1)
Casting the Net (Dunbridge Chronicles 2)
If You Follow Me (Dunbridge Chronicles 3)
Saints and Sailors (Dunbridge Chronicles 4)

Then Sings My Soul

40 reflections on my favourite hymns

Pam Rhodes

MONARCH
BOOKS

Published by Monarch Books
an imprint of
Lion Hudson IP Ltd
Wilkinson House, Jordan Hill Road,
Oxford OX2 8DR, England
Email: monarch@lionhudson.com
www.lionhudson.com/monarch

Hardback ISBN 978 0 85721 720 2
Paperback ISBN 978 0 85721 891 9
e-ISBN 978 0 85721 721 9

First edition 2016

Acknowledgments
Scripture quotations taken from the Holy Bible, New International Version Anglicised. Copyright © 1979, 1984, 2011 Biblica, formerly International Bible Society. Used by permission of Hodder & Stoughton Ltd, an Hachette UK company. All rights reserved. "NIV" is a registered trademark of Biblica. UK trademark number 1448790.

Printed and bound in the UK, October 2017, LH26

A catalogue record for this book is available from the British Library

Agent: Lili Panagi, Panmedia (www.panmediauk.co.uk)

Contents

Introduction

"To sing is to pray twice!"

*T*hat's how the old saying goes – apparently a long-ago quote from St Augustine – and what a lovely thought it is! My years of presenting BBC Television's *Songs of Praise* have provided me with many unforgettable moments of singing much-loved hymns in glorious cathedrals full of Christians. That's the stuff to have the hairs on the back of my neck standing on end! And it makes all the difference in the world when we're not just singing but singing together in praise of God. Hymns are our prayers expressed with love – and for me that adds an extra dimension of feeling and experience that is beyond human explanation.

In fairness, that wonderful quote is not quite what St Augustine meant to say. The line is probably a delightful misquote taken from these words of his which, roughly translated, are:

> For he who sings praise does not only praise, but
> also praises joyfully. He who sings praise not only

*sings, but also loves him to whom he is singing. In
the song of the lover, there is love.*

What I think he meant is that when God is praised in
song, then something happens that takes the song beyond
the ordinary, as if the love with which it is sung is a
manifestation of the love of God himself.

Martin Luther, the sixteenth-century German
reformer and priest whose views formed the basic ethos of
the new Protestant movement that swept across the world
from the start of the sixteenth century, was one of the first
to realize the value of music in worship. We have Luther
to thank for introducing the whole idea of congregational
singing in our churches, even writing around forty verses
to create his own hymnbook. He had long felt that art,
especially music, came from God and should be used in
his service. He wrote:

> *Music is a fair and glorious gift of God. Music
> makes people kinder, gentler, more staid and
> reasonable. I am strongly persuaded that after
> theology, there is no art that can be placed on a
> level with music; for besides theology, music is the
> only art capable of affording peace and joy of the
> heart. The devil flees before the sound of music
> almost as much as before the Word of God.*

I think he's right – and I also think that, just as music can
lift the soul, so too can poetry. Most hymn texts start life

as poems in which the writers pour out their humanity – their fears, pain and worry along with their joy, praise and love – and once their words are partnered with just the right melody, the individual elements fade in the brilliance of the glorious whole. With both words and music forged from love, the result is surely a touching reflection of God's own love for us.

So, in compiling this collection of forty more favourite hymns to follow on from my previous book, *Love So Amazing*, I hope that as you read, your feelings are both of being loved and loving. Most of all, my hope is that you enjoy this storybook about the hymn writers themselves, as well as reading about instances when their hymns have made a deep impact on the hearts of those who found a personal connection with their words, brought alive by music that has added just the right mood and meaning.

And whether St Augustine's quote is correct or not, when it comes to great hymns, I do feel that "to sing is to pray twice". So sing your heart out – in praise and love!

All Creatures of Our God and King

All creatures of our God and king,
Lift up your voice and with us sing
Alleluia, alleluia!
Thou burning sun with golden beam,
Thou silver moon with softer gleam:
O praise him, O praise him,
Alleluia, alleluia, alleluia!

(Based on "Canticle of the Sun" by St Francis of Assisi, 1182–1226)

*Y*ou'd be unlikely to find anyone less like a saint than Francesco Bernardone, whose father was a wealthy merchant who had high hopes of his son taking over his successful business. The spoilt young man loved the trappings of wealth and enjoyed wild parties, but was always aware of his abilities and ambitions to achieve more. He wanted to become a knight, bringing glory and nobility, and finally a call for knights for the

Fourth Crusade gave him a chance to realize his dream. Watched by his proud father as he rode off in a suit of armour decorated with gold and a magnificent cloak, Francis got no further than one day's ride from Assisi. There he dreamed that God told him of his disapproval, and said he must immediately return home. Imagine the shame of going back without ever making it to battle. He was laughed at and called a coward, which was acutely embarrassing for his father.

Francis was uncertain what God wanted of him, so he found a cave in which to pray and to weep for his sins. It wasn't until the young man, who had always led such a protected and cosseted life, met a leper and kissed his hand, even though both his appearance and smell repelled him, that it occurred to Francis that he was being tested by God.

It was when Francis found himself near the ancient church of San Damiano that he heard Christ say, "Repair my church." Taking this literally, Francis took cloth from his father's shop, and sold it to pay for the repairs. Deeply disappointed in his son, his father accused him of theft, publicly demanding that he return the money and renounce all rights as heir to the family fortune.

Francis gave back the money, then stripped off his clothes down to his hair shirt. Wearing nothing but rags, he went off singing. He had nothing and everything. He intended to live by the gospel, in complete simplicity, selling all his possessions, giving all he had to the poor and taking nothing on the journey except the cross. He lived by his belief that poverty was holy. He never intended to found a religious order, but before long he had more than 5,000 followers, celebrating life and serving God by serving others.

We always think of Francis loving creation and nature, and he certainly did. There's a famous story of him preaching to hundreds of birds, that they should be thankful for their beautiful clothes, their freedom and God's care. Another tale is told of him persuading a wolf that had been killing villagers that he should become tame enough to be their pet. But his love was broader than just for nature and animals, because he felt in fellowship with all God's creation. The sparrow was as much his brother as any king or pope.

Just before he died at the age of forty-five, he began to go blind. Blindness was treated at that time by hot irons cauterizing the face. Before the procedure, he asked "Brother Fire" to be kind to him, and reported that he felt nothing at all. However, it was in his blindness that Francis wrote the much loved "Canticle of the Sun", on which the words of this hymn are based. Both they, and the man who wrote them, have been an inspiration to generations of Christians ever since.

Lord, open our eyes to the glory of your creation in all its forms, from the smallest speck of life to the most magnificent. We pray for the wisdom, vision, energy and will to be good stewards of all your gifts, to value everything, and deny our own needs as we recognize the great need of others.

AMEN

All Glory, Laud and Honour

All glory, laud and honour
To thee, Redeemer, King,
To whom the lips of children
Made sweet hosannas ring!

The company of angels
Are praising thee on high,
And mortal flesh and all things
Created make reply.

(Theodulph of Orleans [died 821]; tr. John Mason Neale, 1818–66)

This wonderful Palm Sunday hymn goes back to Palm Sunday in France in the year 821, when Emperor Louis I suspected that Theodulph, Bishop of Orleans, was plotting against him. He threw Theodulph into prison for three years, where the bishop had enough time on his hands to write no fewer than thirty-nine verses for this hymn! Legend has it that on the following Palm Sunday, the king himself passed under the window where Theodulph was singing this hymn as worshippers processed into church. The king was apparently so moved by the sound that he instantly forgave Theodulph and ordered his release; freedom that was short-lived, as Theodulph died later that year.

It's humbling to think that the first thought on the lips of a wronged prisoner like Theodulph should be "glory", but in fact that word is both familiar and comfortable for those of us who are Christians. Just think how many hymns start with the word "glory". Dozens of them!

I suppose it is the perfect word to use in hymns, because "glory" actually covers many different things. The dictionary says it can mean exultation, praise, honour, thanksgiving, adoration and worship, all words which seem absolutely right for people who are trying to explain in human terms how they feel about the God whom they believe has created everything and is master of all. "Glory" can also have a regal ring to it when it means "pomp" or "splendour", much as we might describe the rich pageantry surrounding a monarch, but surely it's even more appropriate when used to describe the colourful ceremonies in our churches where the majesty of God is recognized with reverence and praise. And then "glory" can be resplendent and radiant, like our great cathedrals, where Christians of past generations have poured their craftsmanship, inspiration and devotion into creating beautiful buildings with tall spires that point to heaven.

But while we struggle to express the glory we feel is due to God, we have only to look around us to see how simply God shows his glory to us. Is there anything more glorious than a beautiful sunset, or a country landscape, or an angry sky? Isn't "glorious" the word that comes to mind when you marvel at a newborn baby in your arms, or look beyond the wrinkles of an old person's face to see the wisdom of life etched on their heart? Isn't there glory in the pride you feel as your children take small steps along the path they choose? And how about the patriotic feeling that has your heart thumping when you think of the glory of your homeland?

There is glory all around us – in the grandeur of creation and in the minute detail of each flower, animal, emotion and action. And I sometimes wonder if, when we only think of the grand and splendid, we overlook the everyday pleasures and blessings which are simply wonderful examples of God's glory.

Mind you, when it comes to thinking about the meaning of the word "glory", I once found myself ticking off my grandson about his "gloryhole" of a bedroom, and I wasn't meaning that as a compliment! Isn't the English language odd – but glorious?

May we see your glory in all things, dear Lord – in majesty and in the ordinary, in the resplendent and in the everyday, in the vastness and in the smallest detail. May we never cease to glorify your name and give you thanks for all your blessings.

AMEN

All My Hope on God is Founded

All my hope on God is founded;
He doth still my trust renew.
Me through change and chance he guideth,
Only good and only true.
God unknown, he alone
Calls my heart to be his own.

Still from man to God eternal
Sacrifice of praise be done,
High above all praises praising
For the gift of Christ his Son.
Christ doth call one and all;
Ye who follow shall not fall.

(Robert Bridges, 1844–1930, based on original words by
Joachim Neander, 1650–80)

A couple of summers ago, I compèred a wonderful celebration of rural community life in a centuries-old barn in the beautiful village of Yattendon in Berkshire. For me, with my love of hymns old and new, there was the great thrill of knowing that, around a century before, this village had been home to hymn-writer and Poet Laureate Robert Bridges, who'd retired there after a long career in medicine. Immersing himself in village life, he volunteered to become choirmaster in the little parish church, but soon found himself so frustrated at the poor quality of hymns available to him that he set about compiling *The Yattendon Hymnal*, a collection of his own new hymns, many of which were based on translations of inspirational texts from other languages.

This hymn was one of them, originally written back in the seventeenth century by Joachim Neander, a German pastor with independent and unorthodox opinions which had often got him into trouble before he died from tuberculosis at just thirty years old. Robert Bridges may well have had a good deal of sympathy with the outspoken, sensitive young man who had been a typically rowdy teenager until he went along with a group of friends to make trouble at a religious meeting – and found instead that his life was completely turned around. He became a scholar, and eventually the unordained Reformed Church rector at The Latin School in Dusseldorf, but his religious fervour infuriated the authorities, who insisted he sign a humiliating declaration promising to conform to accepted behaviour. The story goes that he went off to live for months in a cave, where he found consolation in God and nature, writing many of his finest hymn texts there.

One interesting postscript is that Joachim's original family name had been Neumann, "new man" in German, which his grandfather had changed to the Greek form, Neander. With his love of the countryside, Joachim loved the thal (valley) of the Dussel River, which grateful locals renamed Neanderthal after he died. Two centuries later in 1856, it was in that valley that an ancient skeleton was discovered which became known as "the Neanderthal Man". It's a nice thought that a discovery made about the origins of man should be named after a Christian hymn-writer!

Nowadays this hymn is often sung at services such as Remembrance, civic occasions or anniversaries, when we think back with thanks, relief and sometimes sadness over events of previous times, while looking forward in trust and hope to what the future might bring. In today's world, hope can be hard to find, especially where there is so much intolerance, greed and self-seeking, both in nations and individuals. This hymn, though, reminds us that whatever changes and challenges we're faced with, we can safely trust that God is always with us, whether the going is comfortable or filled with difficulty. He knows us, and because he knows our failings as well as our capabilities, we can trust him to guide us "through change and chance". If we're looking for hope, not just for now but forever, what better promise than that?

*Father God, we forget how little we can manage in
our own strength, but it is at times when life is at its
most hard that we need to remember your promise
to us, through Christ. Our reassurance is in you and
the knowledge of your constant presence in every
moment, place, feeling and action. We can trust you,
and in that trust we find all the hope and
promise we need.*

AMEN

Angel Voices, Ever Singing

Angel voices, ever singing,
round thy throne of light,
angel harps, forever ringing,
rest not day or night;
Thousands only live to bless thee,
and confess thee
Lord of might.

(Francis Pott, 1861)

*A*round the middle of the nineteenth century, thousands of parish churches across Britain were busy raising money for a reason that requires our fundraising just as much today! Our church organs are still cherished and valued enough for worshippers to mount major appeals for the renovation they now need, whereas a century and a half ago parishioners were just starting to be swept along with the new trend of installing pipe organs to encourage music and hymn-singing in their church services.

The new fashion certainly put a few noses out of joint, mostly of the minstrels who, until then, had made a good income from leading the singing of metrical psalms on their stringed instruments, usually from the west gallery of the church. The problem was that the same minstrels often played in the local inns over the weekend, so could well turn up for Sunday morning services a little worse for wear! Do you remember rustic musicians like those from the glorious feature films of the Thomas Hardy stories? Well, they quickly fell out of fashion once Victorian churchgoers changed their allegiance to pipe organs – and that is music to the ears of those of us who love to be in church singing traditional hymns with the rich, melodic accompaniment of the organ ringing around the rafters.

When St John the Evangelist Church in Wingates, Lancashire, installed their new pipe organ in 1861, they decided the occasion merited a special dedication service. They were celebrating more than just their new musical acquisition, because at that time the country was going through a great religious revival, along with a flurry of church-building. With their church only two years old, the congregation of St John's felt their new pipe organ was the crowning glory.

Even the vicar was new, and The Reverend Macrorie thought it would help to make the occasion special if he invited his friend, The Reverend Francis Pott, to write a hymn for the dedication service. Once Francis had written the words, he asked a fellow colleague on the committee compiling the new *Hymns Ancient and Modern* hymnbook to compose a suitable tune. Dr Edwin Monk called his melody "Angel Voices", and the words and music immediately created a perfect whole.

As we sing the hymn today, we can still see in verse 3 how Francis gives a hint of the special occasion for which the hymn was written:

> *Thou didst ears and hands and voices*
> *For thy praise design;*
> *Craftsman's art and music's measure*
> *All combine.*

More than that, though, these words capture the spirit of any act of worship where hands, hearts and minds are offered to God in praise.

Most established churches today still make full use of organ music in their services, but increasingly that traditional sound is being replaced by a worship band in which keyboards, drums, guitars, stringed and brass instruments create a very different atmosphere. Most modern Christian songs are now written with that form of accompaniment in mind – and generally congregations love to sing along with them. Over my many years of presenting *Songs of Praise* on BBC Television, I've met so many people worried that the rise of worship bands might have the same effect on the church organ now as those early pipe organs had on the minstrels a century and a half ago.

But worship bands are also looking back to the inspirational words and music of older hymns, then adding rhythm and modern harmonies to make them fresh and easy to sing by congregations of all age groups and denominations. Music has never been so varied and inclusive as it is today, reflecting mood and creating atmosphere to suit every service and occasion.

Lord, we sing your praise. We praise you with our voices and instruments. We give thanks for the composers and writers who have created hymns that inspire, encourage and glorify your name. Lord, just as music lifts our spirits, so we lift our hands and voices to sing your praise.

AMEN

As with Gladness Men of Old

As with gladness men of old
Did the guiding star behold,
As with joy they hailed its light,
Leading onward, beaming bright;
So, most gracious Lord, may we
Evermore your splendour see.

(William Chatterton Dix, 1837–98)

*W*hen William Dix was born the son of a surgeon with literary leanings, no wonder his father's love for the poet Thomas Chatterton was reflected in William's full name! Young William was educated at the local grammar school in Bristol, then went on to become the manager of a marine insurance company in Glasgow. But it seems that, like his father, poetry was in his soul, because in his spare time William was a prolific hymn-writer, publishing no fewer than four volumes of his own hymns.

In addition, he developed a very unusual talent for a boy who grew up in Bristol. He became interested in how

Christianity was observed and celebrated in other parts of the world. The Eastern Orthodox Church was a particular fascination, as well as the church in Abyssinia, and he was responsible for translating into English many hymns and offices from those churches, putting them to music in a form that could also be sung and enjoyed by Christians here.

We're inclined to think of this hymn as a carol, because it's often sung over the Christmas period, but in fact it is an Epiphany hymn, telling the story of the three wise men guided by a bright star to the stable in Bethlehem where Christ had been born. He describes the coming of Christ as a light of the world: beaming, guiding and glorious.

Over Christmas the idea of light becomes very precious to us, reminding us of Christ's light in the twinkling, shining decorations that adorn our homes, shops and streets.

But just as those sparkling lights can make us smile, so others can reflect very different feelings. I remember standing around a Christmas tree in the grounds of our local hospice last year, along with a crowd of people who were all there because the hospice had cared for someone they'd loved and lost, as well as helping family members left behind to cope with their grief. Each glittering candle-shaped light on the tree represented a single life lost, a shining celebration of who they were, what they cared about and why they were so valued. I found it comforting to think the ones I love and miss so much are still glowing now, no longer in pain – out of our sight, but always in our hearts.

It made me think of other occasions when light makes the moment – like birthdays, when candles celebrate the years of our lives as we blow them out surrounded by our friends and family. There's such joy in those candle flames then, shared and heart-warming.

They are in brilliant contrast to the *single* candle I lit in church last Sunday. Then, the flickering light represented a prayer – my prayer of thankfulness for all I have, and my plea for God's care and comfort for those around me whom I love, particularly if they are struggling or in pain.

Whenever we light candles in God's name, we recall the promise and triumph of Christ coming to us as the light of the world. In his light, there is all the remembrance, celebration, sharing, care and comfort of God's love – his brilliant, shining blessing on us all.

Christ, light of the world, shine into our darkness,
guiding us along the right path. May your light live in
our hearts, showing us your way and your will.

AMEN

Be Thou My Guardian and My Guide

Be thou my guardian and my guide,
And hear me when I call;
Let not my slippery footsteps slide,
And hold me lest I fall.

And if I tempted am to sin,
And outward things are strong,
Do thou, O Lord, keep watch within,
And save my soul from wrong.

(Isaac Williams, 1802–65)

It was a very significant day in Isaac Williams' life when, in 1823, he won the prestigious Latin prize at Oxford University's Trinity College, not least because it was the proper start of his friendship with the man he came to think of as both his tutor and his spiritual mentor, John Keble. Along with John Henry Newman, John Keble was a leading light in the Oxford Movement, with its aims to move the Church of England closer to its Catholic roots. In the years that followed, Isaac travelled the same path, except that where the other two excelled in intellect and as orators, Isaac is said to have had a common-sense view of the movement's aims. One supporter said, "We have too much sail, and we want ballast." Isaac Williams was the ballast.

Most of us remember this hymn from our childhood, particularly around Lent when the words always seem so apt as we recall the forty days and nights Christ spent in the desert being tempted and tested. Many of us echo Christ's experience in a small way in our own lives by giving up something we really love – like chocolate, for instance – then hope we can resist the temptation to have a quick bite of Fruit 'n' Nut while no one's looking!

I can resist chocolate, but not liquorice allsorts! I love them. I gave them up once when we *all* started a diet after Christmas, and I can't tell you how often I found myself looking longingly at them in the supermarket. If I had given in to temptation and munched a packet of liquorice allsorts, what harm would it have done? I'd have hated myself for being weak. I wouldn't have been able to look in the mirror because I'd have felt fat; but the only person I'd have damaged would be me. I could forgive myself for that.

I wonder what would be a worse sort of temptation to give in to. Gossip, perhaps, when we're told something private, and asked to keep it secret? The trouble is that sometimes other people's secrets can become such a burden that the knowledge is too much to bear, and there's an overwhelming temptation to tell someone we can trust to keep it to themselves! But of course, they might feel tempted to pass it on too, and before long it's not a secret any more. Then we've betrayed the trust of a friend and hurt them badly in the process – and all because we gave in to temptation in a way that is completely unforgivable.

During his time in the desert, Jesus wasn't only tempted in the most persuasive way, but his resolve was tested to the extreme. Christians in this country are quite comfortable really, but there are millions of Christians elsewhere in the world who are persecuted for their faith, to the point of death if they are not prepared to deny what they believe. If your life, or the safety of your family, were in danger, of course you'd be tempted to say or do whatever was needed to avoid pain and hardship! And yet so many brave Christians stay resolute and still refuse to comply.

To resist such temptation is not only courageous, it's truly humbling. If they can stand firm, then the least I can do is resist petty temptations like gossip or chocolate.

Liquorice allsorts, though – I might have to work on that…

Christ our Lord, in the desert you were taunted and tempted, but remained true and resolute. Be with us in our lack of resolution. Lead us not into temptation, Lord, but if we are faced with a choice of whether to take an easy path that we know to be wrong, we pray for the strength to resist and the courage to refuse.

AMEN

Breathe on Me, Breath of God

Breathe on me, breath of God,
Fill me with life anew,
That I may love what thou dost love,
And do what thou wouldst do.

(Edwin Hatch, 1835–89)

*E*dwin Hatch was an academic who may have written many papers in his time, but only penned this one hymn, as far as we know. He wrote it for what he thought of as Whitsuntide, which others will recognize as the time in the Christian calendar when we remember Pentecost. That is when Christians recall the coming of the Holy Spirit to Christ's disciples just a few weeks after his death and resurrection, thus establishing not just the practical start of God's church on earth, but his spiritual church in the hearts of all who follow him. In this hymn, Edwin Hatch has captured the responsibility that discipleship places on us all. He prays that we will love as God would love, and do what he would do.

In recent times, we have all marked the end of the Second World War in Europe, which inevitably brings back awful images of how liberation finally came to the prisoners, mostly Jewish, who were rescued from Hitler's inhuman concentration camps. Some years ago, I had the company of Jonathan Sachs, at that time the Chief Rabbi of Britain, as we went round the Holocaust Exhibition at the Imperial War Museum in London. The photos and relics on show were deeply distressing, so I asked him, "Six million killed, people of faith. Where was God?" And his answer has stayed with me. "The question is not 'Where was *God*?', but 'Where was *man*?'"

When I think of that now, it takes me back to when I was a youngster living on an estate where all the houses circled an area of grass that was a playground for kids, watched by parents in every household. One day there was great upset when a bossy boy pinched a smaller lad's bike and ended up buckling the wheel. The bike's owner immediately burst into tears, but then we all knew him to be a cry baby, so we just watched from the sidelines as the big boy taunted him.

Suddenly, into the crowd marched Nan, our formidable grandmother. One by one, she asked us all what we thought of the big boy, and eventually the word "bully" was mentioned by just about everyone. When she looked at the smaller boy, we told her he was *always* a cry baby, so she asked us why he cried so often, and what we knew about him that might make him unhappy. And we *did* know – that his dad had died, so his mum was bringing up four children on her own; that they all shared hand-me-downs we often made fun of; and that the only bike we'd ever seen any of them use was the one that was now broken in front of us.

We felt so ashamed. Then Nan said, "Every single one of us is shaped by our circumstances, and unless you can imagine yourself in *his* shoes and understand what he's been through and how he's feeling, you've no right to judge or bully. And you lot standing around are just as bad! You knew something wrong was happening and you did nothing. That makes you no better than that bully!"

I often think of her words these days when there's so much bullying going on around the world. Because I think the problems are too huge for my opinion to matter, I see myself standing back watching what I know to be wrong – and doing nothing.

I can't blame God for that. That's down to me. I'm glad Nan can't see me now...

Father, as Christians, we are called to love as you love and try to do what you would do, but we fail so often. When we know something is wrong, it's not enough to do nothing. Give us the courage and wisdom to recognize your will and follow it.

AMEN

Come, Thou Fount of Every Blessing

Come, thou Fount of every blessing,
Tune my heart to sing thy grace;
Streams of mercy, never ceasing,
Call for songs of loudest praise.
Teach me some melodious sonnet
Sung by flaming tongues above;
Praise the mount! I'm fixed upon it,
Mount of thy redeeming love.

(Robert Robinson, 1735–90)

The writer of this hymn, Robert Robinson, might have had a very comfortable life if his mother, Mary Wilkin, hadn't disappointed her genteel East Anglian family by marrying a lowly customs officer, Michael Robinson. Robert's father died when he was still a small boy, but even that didn't soften his wealthy grandfather's heart, as he disinherited his grandson with a settlement sum of just ten shillings and sixpence. His mother was left struggling to make ends meet, eventually sending her fourteen-year-old son to London to learn the trade of a barber.

London life turned the country boy's head, and before long he fell in with what his mother would describe as definitely the wrong sort of company. There's a story that, on one occasion, the drunken gang barged into where a gypsy was telling fortunes, and demanded to be told theirs for free. The gypsy was well used to dealing with difficult teenagers, but before they left, she pointed to Robert and told him he would live long enough to see both his children and his grandchildren. Her words haunted him because, for the first time, he realized that if he had a future of responsibility ahead of him, he'd have to change his ways.

Not long after, he and the gang decided to gatecrash an open air service led by a great friend of the Wesleys, George Whitefield. Robert's plans to disrupt and heckle were scuppered as he began to listen to George's sermon, which he felt was aimed directly at him. By the age of twenty-three, Robert had become a minister himself, appointed by John Wesley to run the Methodist chapel where his family lived in the Suffolk town of Mildenhall. It was there, for Pentecost in 1858, that he penned the words of this hymn.

In the third verse, he included these prophetic lines:

> *Prone to wander, Lord, I feel it,*
> *Prone to leave the God I love.*

As time went on, Robert slipped away from his

commitment to faith, lapsing into questionable behaviour and friendships which plainly troubled him, although he didn't seem able to pull back. The words of his text show that he was aware of his own weakness.

One day, when he happened to be riding in a stagecoach with a lady who, he realized, was humming this hymn, he was so moved he started to cry. Anxiously, she asked him what was the matter, and he replied that he was "the poor unhappy man who wrote that hymn many years ago, and I would give a thousand worlds, if I had them, to enjoy the feelings I had then".

The previous lines in his hymn tell of his deep longing to be drawn back into God's loving care:

> *Let thy goodness like a fetter*
> *Bind my wand'ring heart to thee.*

That's a feeling many of us can identify with – our heartfelt prayer for God's guidance and protection at times when we feel we're taking the wrong path, making unwise decisions, or not relating to those around us with the care and respect we would wish for ourselves. Like Robert Robinson, we all behave selfishly at times, and are filled with regret. It's occasions like that when we need, as the great gospel hymn-writer Fanny Crosby would say, to "take it to the Lord in prayer"!

How easy it is to lose our way, O God. In spite of

good intentions, there are times when we're all guilty of putting ourselves first and disregarding the needs of others. Christ understood our failings and wrong-doings so well that he gave his life for us on the cross. Since he did that for us, may we never fail to be grateful, and determined to commit ourselves wholeheartedly to his will.

AMEN

Come, Ye Thankful People, Come

Come, ye thankful people, come,
Raise the song of harvest-home!
All be safely gathered in
Ere the winter storms begin;
God, our Maker, doth provide
For our wants to be supplied;
Come to God's own temple, come,
Raise the song of harvest-home!

(Henry Alford, 1810–71)

I am including this hymn, not because of the author, Henry Alford, who was a rather serious-minded Christian academic, but because of his contemporary, Robert Hawker (1803–75), whose endearingly odd, quixotic personality added an eccentric dimension to his role as parish priest in the small village of Morwenstow on the Cornish coast. It was hardly a plum posting. No vicar had offered to be in residency there for more than a century. But growing up as the son of a relatively local curate, this was a church Robert had loved for years.

Songs of Praise sent me down to record a programme there some years ago, and I really warmed to the stories of Robert, who was said to stride around in his favourite pink fez and a poncho made from a yellow horse blanket. There were tales of him in his long claret-coloured coat, silver hair streaming in the wind as he pleaded with reluctant lifeboat men to save the crew of yet another wrecked ship. He tried tempting them with bottles of whisky, and sometimes drove off to fetch the lifeboat himself – but, to his disgust, the men would only set out once the ship had been scuppered and legally available for salvage. Later, the bodies would be brought up the cliff on broken planks to the church where Robert, unsure of the faith of the victims, would hold his own burial ritual blending the Prayer Book with what he imagined was the practice of the early Cornish saints.

He certainly had a sense of humour – like the time he swam out to perch on a rock wearing a wig plaited with seaweed, combing his hair and wailing like a mermaid. And the vicarage he built himself was almost a folly, with chimneys fashioned to look like the towers of churches he'd loved. He was happily married twice – first to a woman twenty years older than himself, who supported him through his studies; then, at the age of sixty, to a twenty-year-old, who gave him three daughters – and a lot of money problems! By that time, perhaps not surprisingly, he increasingly suffered from bouts of depression, at one time eating nothing but clotted cream!

But it was in 1843 that this wonderfully charismatic man pinned up a notice announcing a special service in which the old custom of making Eucharistic bread from the first corn would be revived:

> *Let us gather together in the chancel of our*
> *church, and there receive, in the bread of the new*
> *corn, that blessed sacrament which was ordained*
> *to strengthen and refresh our souls.*

Perhaps, in this first known Christian service to give thanks for the harvest, his congregation sang the new hymn "Come, Ye Thankful People, Come", written by Henry Alford – or even "We Plough the Fields, and Scatter", which had been recently translated from its original German. Certainly, although Christians have always given thanks for the harvest, it wasn't until Robert Hawker devised his harvest festival that this popular celebration found its place in our Christian calendar.

I remember sitting in Robert's tiny hut built out of shipwreck flotsam, perched on the cliff-top looking out to sea. They say every man needs a shed. This was his, where he prayed, wrote, sang and let his fertile mind roam free.

At times, the established church can be a little stuffy and inflexible. It needs free spirits like Robert, full of imagination and passion – or, as Archbishop Michael

Ramsey described him a hundred years later, "a beyond man in a beyond place".

Lord, let the fresh air of your creation blow through our worship and our faith. And may we recognize the richness of other people's ideas, breathing fresh life into our understanding of you and our love for one another.

AMEN

Day by Day

Day by day, and with each passing moment,
Strength I find to meet my trials here;
Trusting in my Father's wise bestowment,
I've no cause for worry or for fear.
He, whose heart is kind beyond all measure,
Gives unto each day what he deems best,
Lovingly its part of pain and pleasure,
Mingling toil with peace and rest.

(Lina Sandell, 1832–1903)

An inevitable part of the human experience is that just as we have times of joy, health and comfort, so we also have the overwhelming exhaustion of sadness, fear and worry. This hymn came from the pen of a Swedish woman who had known the most terrible grief, so her words, born from pain, speak to the very soul of others who are suffering.

Lina grew up in the most loving of homes, the daughter of a Lutheran pastor of the little church in Fröderyd, Sweden. She was a "daddy's girl", loving her father's company, whether she was following him around the parish or playing on the floor of his study while he worked. Their love was severely tested when Lina developed a childhood paralysis which doctors suspected was incurable. Whether it was medical treatment that finally brought her through, or the intense prayer of both the family and their congregation, Lina recovered to become known across Scandinavia as one of the most influential writers of the late nineteenth century.

That influence came not from prose or articles, but from her hymn texts, of which there were about 600 in all. They touched the heart of the nation, because they flowed from her own broken heart. When she was twenty-six years old, she was travelling with her father to Gothenburg on a boat crossing Lake Vättern. Suddenly, the boat lurched and Lina watched helplessly as her father was thrown overboard and drowned in the water below her.

Nothing could have prepared her for such an unexpected tragedy. Her grief was so deep that it could have destroyed her and yet, as she emerged from the experience, it was clear that her faith had not only supported her throughout, but was stronger than ever. She had always written hymns, but from then on her verses had an added depth and sensitivity. Just look at the words of this first verse, in which she acknowledges the "trials", "worry", "pain" and "toil" of everyday life, but assures us she can face them all by trusting in God's kind and loving heart to give her the strength she needs.

Her fame spread once her writing was discovered by a man known in Sweden as the "spiritual troubadour". Oscar Ahnfelt had a wonderful talent for writing beautiful but simple melodies which had people joining in wherever he travelled, accompanying the songs with his ten-string guitar. Lina said, "Ahnfelt has sung my songs into the hearts of the people," as she set about writing yet more lyrics to match his music.

Ahnfelt's preaching was part of the wave of religious revival which swept across Scandinavia, to the concern of the authorities, who threatened him with a royal injunction. Finally, King Karl XV himself summoned Ahnfelt to sing for him, and when he heard his music accompanying Lina's words, the king was deeply moved, saying, "You may sing as much as you desire in both of my kingdoms!"

In the depths of grief and pain, it's often hard to find just the right line of encouragement that you know is *somewhere* in the Bible – and even harder to put into your own words of prayer the torture of your suffering and your desperate need. Lina understood that pain, and in this simple hymn has provided the prayerful comfort and reassurance longed for by those who are hurting.

Then Sings My Soul

**In the darkest times, Christ is with us. In our pain,
Christ holds out his arms in unconditional love. Draw
us to you, Lord. Be with us always.**

AMEN

Father, Lead Me Day by Day

Father, lead me day by day
Ever in thine own good way;
Teach me to be pure and true,
Show me what I ought to do.

When in danger, make me brave;
Make me know that thou canst save,
Keep me safe by thy dear side,
Let me in thy love abide.

(John Page Hopps, 1834–1911)

I don't know if John Page Hopps was a dad, but I hope so. He obviously loved children, because although he wrote many lofty, serious sermons and hymns, he also compiled one hymnbook specially for children, and another for young people. So I hope that he combined his role as a spiritual father and guide to parishioners in Birmingham, Sheffield, Glasgow, Leicester and London with being a much loved father within his own family.

As he died in 1911, he never knew that by the 1970s there would be a special day in the year dedicated to fathers. He would have been familiar with the idea of Mothering Sunday within the Christian calendar, always falling on the fourth Sunday of Lent. Father's Day, though, is a relative newcomer. It was an idea that occurred to an American lady called Sonora Dodd, as she listened to a Mother's Day sermon in 1909. She wondered why there shouldn't be a day to honour fathers just as we honour mothers – especially as her own father, who'd been a veteran of the Civil War, became a single dad, taking on the care of Sonora and her five brothers and sisters after his wife died in childbirth.

It took a while for the idea to catch on, with the help of a few trade groups who manufactured ties, tobacco pipes and other traditional gifts for fathers at the time. Eventually, in the early seventies, Father's Day was made official in the States, quickly catching on here.

I'd have liked a special day to show my father how much he was loved and appreciated, but he died when I was just fourteen, so I feel now as if I hardly knew him. I remember him being a bit stern, rather remote as he was often away for work, but I also remember him singing daft songs and kicking a ball about with us. I never had chance, though, to know him as an adult – what music he liked; what he laughed at; what team he supported. Was he a good driver? Would he have approved of me?

I often catch sight of myself in the mirror and see his face in mine. Made in his image, this man I hardly knew.

It's that thought that's made me realize how much I really want to get to *know* God, because we talk about him as a father. I can still picture the image I had of God from the Bible stories I was told as a child – powerful, forbidding, judgmental, aware of our failings – a bit like my dad, who seemed so stern and remote all those years ago. But I also remember my mum saying how loving and supportive Dad was, giving us parameters on how to behave, so that we would always treat others with respect, and make the most of all the gifts and talents we'd been blessed with. I suppose today it would be called "tough love", and that's a good way to describe the relationship I feel God has with me – *tough* because of the parameters he sets for how I should live and treat other people, but also understanding, forgiving and infinitely loving.

Father, you said that unless we become like little children, we will never enter the kingdom of heaven. With your loving example, may we respect and learn from our parents, and in time become good parents ourselves. We pray for your care, protection and guidance, dear Father, now and always.

AMEN

Forth in Thy Name, O Lord, I Go

Forth in thy name, O Lord, I go,
My daily labour to pursue;
Thee, only thee, resolved to know
In all I think or speak or do.

(Charles Wesley, 1707–88)

*C*harles Wesley certainly knew about "daily labour". Just looking at the long list of hymns he wrote, journeys he made, places he visited, issues he fought for and people whose lives he touched, I can't help wondering if he ever found time to sleep! But he seemed to have so much he wanted to say and achieve, I imagine he didn't mind hard work at all when it was directed towards a goal that was dear to his heart.

It's not as if he spent hours in a comfortable study as he wrote his 8,000 or so hymn texts. The Wesley brothers covered around a quarter of a million miles, preaching across the length and breadth of Britain. You can just picture the Wesley band of pilgrims on the road, sharing not just their faith but other more domestic issues – like family commitments, worry about money or security, difficult relationships, sore feet – all the very human things, in fact, that might well worry any of us today.

Charles didn't always accompany his brother John, but no journey was without challenge. Sometimes they rode on horseback. Sometimes they walked for miles on end, unsure whether they'd find a welcome. People were very suspicious of these itinerant preachers who challenged the way they worshipped, and they often made their feelings clear by driving the visitors away with sticks and insults.

Not only that, but even if there was a crowd waiting to hear them preach and sing, can you imagine the practical problems involved in making sure everyone could hear? Wouldn't they have loved the idea of having a microphone! Instead, it must only have been the people lucky enough, or perhaps with the sharpest elbows, who would have been able to hear properly – and those further back, who were struggling to catch not just their words but the meaning too, might well have got disgruntled or bored, and wandered away.

We're also inclined to think that the melodies to which we sing Charles Wesley's hymns would have been the same then as they are now, but actually, with Charles writing so many verses every day, it was hard to find melodies of the time for all the new titles. In the open air, it was rare to have anything like a piano or organ on hand to provide accompaniment, so often there would have been the most basic of musical instruments, or none at all, to lead melodies that mostly the crowd had never heard before.

But in spite of all the challenges, people did come in droves to listen to the Wesley brothers, so it must have been the power of their preaching and the deep sincerity of their mission that really moved and inspired them. Perhaps it was also the fact that just as John's preaching was rooted in the Bible, so too were Charles's hymns. I always find it amazing that even though his verses are so beautiful and poetic, in almost every line there is a definite biblical reference. His knowledge of the Bible, and his real understanding of the meaning of those lines of Scripture and their relevance to us in our everyday lives, made his hymns increasingly popular with their followers at the time, and even more appreciated and loved now in our generation.

How many of us, Lord, fit our worship and faith into convenient pockets in our lives? How different from the old-time preachers, like the Wesley brothers and many others, who took the road facing hardship and insult in order to spread the message of the gospel. Help us to live out our faith, Lord, not just on Sunday, but in every second of our lives.

AMEN

Guide Me, O Thou Great Jehovah

Guide me, O thou great Jehovah,
Pilgrim through this barren land;
I am weak, but thou art mighty,
Hold me with thy powerful hand:
Bread of heaven, bread of heaven,
Feed me till I want no more,
Feed me till I want no more.

(William Williams, 1717–91)

As the son of a prosperous farmer in Wales, William Williams had always intended to become a doctor – until the day he went along to an open-air revival meeting at which evangelist Howell Harris, a fellow Welshman, was preaching. Young Williams left that meeting a changed man. He took to the road, travelling nearly 100,000 miles during his forty-three years of ministry, often finding crowds of 10,000 or more waiting to hear him preach.

Those crowds came to sing his songs too, which is

not surprising when Wales is universally known as the land of song. Over the years William earned himself a nickname as "the sweet singer of Wales", writing more than 800 hymns during his lifetime. This hymn, above all others, is his most famous, thought of today almost as a national anthem for Wales, as well as being a great favourite with Christians around the world.

The words are based on the biblical story of the Israelites' flight from Egypt to Canaan on a journey that lasted forty years. God provided for the travellers with a daily supply of fresh manna, a pillar of cloud by day and fire by night to guide them in the right direction, and a fountain of water at times of drought, when Moses struck a large rock with his wooden staff.

William describes the travellers as pilgrims, and in recent years I've been lucky enough to join other pilgrims on some truly inspirational journeys of faith. We've been on trips around the Mediterranean, visiting places where St Paul spent time 2,000 years ago, and it was really emotional to think *we* were in that amphitheatre in Ephesus where he stood to preach, in the town where he wrote letters with encouraging words that are still so familiar to us today. We've cruised around the British Isles, calling at the islands where saints such as Cuthbert and Aidan forged the start of Christian belief across this country. And we've been in the Holy Land, visiting places with names from the Bible that we've known ever since we can remember. To actually *be* there – in Bethlehem where Christ was born, by the River Jordan where he was baptized, or in Gethsemane where he prepared for his crucifixion – is unbelievably moving.

But looking back, the real pilgrimage was not so much about where we went, but about what we shared along the way with our fellow pilgrims. My warmest memories are of when we were just enjoying each other's company, laughing, praying, singing, eating – or simply worn out! And as we travelled, we found we had chance to talk, *really* talk, about things that worried or challenged us. It's an odd truth that often it's easier to share our most private feelings when we're away from home, able to confide in our companions who may be strangers at the start of our journey, but who become dear friends by the time we part company.

Isn't the same true of life itself? Whatever path that journey takes you down, it's the friends you meet, the people you love and the faith you share that truly warm your heart.

Father, may we be pilgrims together and friends to all as we travel along our journey of life. Help us to be good comrades and caring friends. Bless us as we go, and welcome us when we finally reach our home in you.

AMEN

Hail to the Lord's Anointed

Hail to the Lord's Anointed!
Great David's greater Son;
Hail, in the time appointed,
His reign on earth begun!
He comes to break oppression,
To set the captive free;
To take away transgression,
And rule in equity.

(James Montgomery, 1771–1854)

When you see who wrote these words, it's no surprise that within the first few lines James Montgomery is already talking about setting captives free and equal rule for all! Whenever he saw injustice, he spoke out, and his forthright opinions landed him in prison more than once.

James was born into a family of Moravians, a relatively small religious sect to which John and Charles Wesley owed their conversion. James's father was an

Irish peasant who settled in Scotland after becoming a Moravian pastor. When their son was just five years old, his parents felt they were called to work in the West Indies, ministering to slaves on the sugar plantations. James never saw them again, because it wasn't long before they both lost their lives there.

That left the boy stranded in the Moravian Fulneck seminary in Yorkshire, where he never really settled, because he was a poet by nature, and poetry was banned at Fulneck. He left school to become a baker and shopkeeper, and finally took up a post in Sheffield as assistant to Joseph Gales, a well-known bookseller and printer of *The Sheffield Register* newspaper. *The Register* was famous for its extreme political views – so extreme that when Gales was forced to flee the country, twenty-three-year-old James took charge of the paper. He changed its name to *The Sheffield Iris*, but there was no change in the way it championed causes close to his heart – like the teaching of writing in Sunday schools (which the authorities felt would instil dangerous ideas into working-class young people!), and the abolition of slavery and the practice of using climbing-boys by chimney sweeps. He believed in democratic principles, especially those expressed through revolution, and it was when he wrote an impassioned account of the storming of the Bastille that he first ended up in prison, with his equally outspoken account of a reform riot in Sheffield resulting in his second spell in jail a few years later.

Moving on from his Moravian roots, James became interested first in the Wesleyan Society, then later began to worship as an Anglican. One of the reasons for this was his love of writing hymns, about 400 in all. Many years earlier in Germany, Martin Luther had introduced congregational singing. Isaac Watts had written hundreds of hymns for non-conforming English churches, and Charles Wesley had done much the same for the Methodists. Frustrated that only the chanting of psalms was allowed in the Church of England, James joined forces with The Reverend Thomas Cotterill to produce a new hymnbook for his Anglican congregation. The reaction was varied. Some stalwarts were convinced that singing hymns was un-Anglican, so they dredged up an ancient law prohibiting the singing in church of hymns of "human composure" – only psalms were considered proper. The church courts upheld the law banning hymn-singing, but the Archbishop of York later repealed that decision so that in 1821 hymns were finally allowed in the Church of England.

Martin Luther once held up a Bible, saying, "This is the gospel." Then he held up a hymnbook and said, "And this is how we remember it." James understood that, and applied his usual determination to fight for what he believed to be right. In doing so, he paved the way for the fellowship of hymn-singing which we take for granted today.

We never really know, Lord, how our actions today may bring benefit and opportunity to others tomorrow. And our lack of action now may make difficult times even more challenging for others whom we never know. Help us always to recognize what is right, and to work in your strength for justice and freedom.

AMEN

Hark! The Herald Angels Sing

Hark! The herald angels sing
"Glory to the new-born king,
Peace on earth and mercy mild,
God and sinners reconciled."
Joyful, all ye nations rise,
Join the triumph of the skies;
With the angelic host proclaim,
"Christ is born in Bethlehem."
Hark! The herald angels sing
"Glory to the new-born King."

(Charles Wesley, 1707–88)

My nan had a wealth of sayings she could come out with as a comment on any situation. "If you want something done properly, do it yourself!" was one of her favourites, but if her advice had been taken when this carol first saw the light of day, it most certainly would not have pride of place at every Christmas service, as it does today. If ever there was a hymn that benefited from teamwork, this is it!

Among his 8,000 or so hymn texts, Charles Wesley wrote many that marked the seasons of the Christian calendar. When these verses first appeared as a "Hymn for Christmas Day" in the 1739 Wesley hymnbook called *Hymns and Sacred Poems*, it started with the line "Hark how all the welkin rings". "Welkin" was an old word to describe the sky, the vault of heaven – and that is where the next contributor to the finished carol came in. One of the Wesley team, George Whitefield, plainly didn't think that word felt right, so he changed the opening line to the now familiar "Hark! The herald angels sing".

Then, just over forty years after the original text was written, Tate and Brady came out with a new version of their hymnbook, in which they included this carol, adding their own two lines of chorus, which Charles had never envisaged himself. What Charles *had* made clear was that he wanted a particular style of music to be matched with this text, something slow and sombre, befitting the grandeur of his words. He might well have turned in his grave, then, if he'd known how a spark of genius by an English organist led to a melody being partnered with his words in a way that he would have thought most unbecoming!

A century after Charles wrote his text, Felix Mendelssohn composed a cantata to mark Johann Gutenberg's invention of the printing press. At the time, Mendelssohn commented that he didn't mind how else the melody was used, as long as it wasn't partnered with sacred words. Fifteen years later, organist William Cummings realized that Mendelssohn's tune fitted Wesley's words perfectly – and he was right, because that partnership propelled this carol to become one of the most loved in the world. Neither the composer nor the author would have approved – but we definitely do!

My nan did have a point, though, that sometimes, if you alone have a vision of what's needed, it's better to undertake every step of the work yourself rather than find that the finished article is not really what you had in mind. It is also true that none of us have a monopoly on what's right, or on good ideas – and often the spark of a concept by one person can be enhanced and built upon by others until the finished whole is worth so much more than the sum of the individual parts.

The "team" involved in creating this carol all lived in different times and places, but I can't help wondering what they would have come up with if they could have been in one room, pooling all their experience and skills to write this carol. Could they ever have agreed? Or was there a little divine help given to each of them over the years that led to the existence of this glorious hymn of praise to mark the birth of Christ?

Father, we celebrate the coming of Christ to our world as a baby in Bethlehem with joyful carols that give thanks for the promise and glory of his birth. We sing as ourselves, unique and individual – and we sing as a congregation, sharing our contribution to the life of our church and the blessing of our faith. Use us in all ways, dear Lord, giving of ourselves as well as working with others.

AMEN

Holy, Holy, Holy

Holy, holy, holy! Lord God Almighty!
Early in the morning our song shall rise to thee;
Holy, holy, holy! Merciful and mighty,
God in three Persons, blessed Trinity!

Holy, holy, holy! Though the darkness hide thee,
Though the eye of sinful man thy glory may not see,
Only thou art holy, there is none beside thee
Perfect in power, in love and purity.

(Reginald Heber, 1783–1826)

While he was vicar in the country town of Hodnet in Shropshire, Reginald Heber set about writing a hymn for each of the solemn days, feast days and ordinary Sundays in the Church of England calendar. Although this shows his love of hymns and his understanding of how much they can contribute to our worship, he was very fastidious in his approach to writing, as we can guess from this intriguing comment of his:

*I avoid all fulsome, indecorous or erotic language
to Him whom no unclean lips dare approach.*

This hymn was originally written with Trinity Sunday in
mind, while over the years it has graced many a school
assembly because of the line in the first verse which
suggests it is just right for "early morning" worship.
However, I'm sure I'm not alone in loving this hymn
because of its perfect partnering with John Bacchus
Dykes' melody *Nicaea*, which creates a mood of deep
holiness.

When I think about holiness today, I find myself
challenged by the thought of all those saints from long
ago whose lives were totally devoted to God. They turned
their backs on any sense of comfort, left their families,
their professions and often the company of anyone else
at all in order to live in pure and humble poverty. Some
lived as hermits, cut off completely from the world.
Others travelled the length and breadth of the country
to spread the Christian message, often to be faced with
violent resistance. Many met an untimely end in the most
horrific way as they sacrificed their lives for their faith.
And frankly, however devoted we are to God, if that's
holiness, well, I don't fancy trying it!

But surely, to have a sense of holiness in your life
doesn't mean you have to be saintlike, denying yourself
ordinary pleasures in order to prove your devotion.

After all, I think God made each one of us unique and individual, and blessed with life in abundance. He knows that sometimes we stumble and fail. He knows we need his forgiveness, guidance and protection. But I believe he wants us to become everything we should be, and live life to the full. Just think about the everyday things that bring us satisfaction and fulfilment: loving relationships with family and friends; being a parent; enjoying our work; expressing a talent; achieving an ambition; appreciating beauty in the world around us. All these are gifts from God, and opportunities to be all we can be.

So perhaps we don't have to behave perfectly to have a place for holiness in our lives. We just have to present ourselves to God as we are – as he knows us, warts and all – and allow ourselves moments throughout our day when we acknowledge his presence, his goodness and his love.

I like to spend a bit of time in the morning before everyone else surfaces to dedicate the day ahead. I often find a prayer in my mind as I watch the breakfast news, or as I catch the train to London or dash round the supermarket before returning home in the evening. And I always end my day by sharing with God the small triumphs, the big worries, my hopes and prayers for others, and my thanks for his unfailing love.

You don't have to be a saint to need a bit of holiness in your life.

With so many responsibilities, concerns and busyness in our daily lives, dearest Lord, it is easy to overlook our deep need of your Holy Spirit in all we do. Help us to find holiness in every place, action and person. Wherever we stand, may we think of that place as holy ground. Whatever our thoughts, may they be turned to you in humble prayer.

AMEN

I Need Thee Every Hour

I need thee every hour,
Most gracious Lord;
No tender voice like thine
Can peace afford.

I need thee, O I need thee!
Every hour I need thee:
O bless me now my Saviour!
I come to thee.

(Annie Sherwood Hawks, 1835–1918)

Bearing in mind how intensely personal the wording of hymn texts can be, often written at times that are deeply worrying or sad, it's perhaps a little surprising that one of the most poignant and touching hymns of all should have been written for the most practical of reasons.

Annie Sherwood Hawks was born in the New York area and then married there. She'd enjoyed writing poetry from a very early age, even having one piece published in a newspaper when she was only fourteen. Ten years later, when she and her new husband moved to Brooklyn, they joined a church where the pastor happened to be the renowned hymn-writer and composer Robert Lowry. Robert soon recognized Annie's talent for writing, and to encourage her he challenged that if she wrote the words, he would write the music, which was too good an opportunity for Annie to miss.

Inspiration came to her one June day when, as she later described, she became "filled with the sense of the nearness of my Master", so much so that she found herself wondering how anyone could live without him, in either joy or pain. "Suddenly," she continued, "the words *I need thee every hour* flashed into my mind, and very quickly the thought had full possession of me."

Once Robert had added the melody, the new hymn was first performed at the National Sunday School Convention in Cincinnati, Ohio, in 1872. Immediately it became clear that the words had a deep effect on those who were going through particularly harrowing times, which rather surprised Annie, as she'd written it so quickly and simply.

"For myself," she said, "the hymn was prophetic rather than expressive of my own experiences, for it was wafted out to the world on the wings of love and joy, instead of under the stress of personal sorrow."

It wasn't until she herself had been touched by personal sorrow following the death of her husband that she began to appreciate why others found her words so powerful.

> *At first I did not understand why the hymn so greatly touched the throbbing heart of humanity. Years later, however, under the shadow of a great loss, I came to understand something of the comforting power of the words I had been permitted to give out to others in my hours of sweet serenity and peace.*

One thing I've learned from years of meeting people through *Songs of Praise* is that often unnoticed comments or moments during the broadcast can have a profound effect on someone watching at home. Sometimes, one of the people sharing their testimony says something that strikes a chord with a viewer. Maybe it's the line of a reading or hymn that puts into simple and poetic words exactly what they've been feeling. Many times I've heard from a son or daughter who shared with me how their mum had been especially moved by a line she'd heard on the programme, and then closed her eyes for the final time as she listened to one of her favourite hymns that followed.

Writers don't always recognize the power of their words, but down the ages Christian writers have spoken of verses that almost seemed to write themselves, as if by divine power. Many hymn lines in particular are so profound in the impact they make that, although they may have been penned by human hand, it certainly feels as if they came straight from the heart of God.

In joy, in pain, in trouble or challenge, I need thee, Lord. Every moment, every place, bless me now and always, my Saviour.

AMEN

I Stand Amazed in the Presence

*I stand amazed in the presence
Of Jesus the Nazarene,
And wonder how he could love me,
A sinner condemned, unclean.*

*How marvellous! How wonderful!
And my song shall ever be:
How marvellous! How wonderful
Is my Saviour's love for me!*

(Words and music by Charles Gabriel, 1856–1932)

A young lad from a farming family near the prairie
town of Wilton in the middle of Iowa was hardly
likely to become one of the most prolific composers of
gospel songs of all time, but Charles Gabriel was born with
such a passion for music that his talent quickly outgrew
his upbringing. When no formal lessons were available,
he set about teaching himself to play the family's reed
organ, picking out his own melodies on the keyboard
and adding words to create hymns and songs. There's a

lovely story of the local pastor stopping in the street to ask young Charles if he had any ideas about what hymn might go with his sermon topic for the following Sunday. Within a couple of days, the boy had produced a finished song which, like all the rest of the 8,000 or so hymns he eventually wrote, was packed full of gospel messages and really enjoyable to sing!

After setting up singing schools in various locations around the area, Charles's talent was recognized by the Grace Methodist Episcopal Church in San Francisco, and they invited him to become their music director. Two years as music director there provided him with the opportunity for plenty of hymn-writing, and that eventually led to him being taken on in 1912 by Homer Rodeheaver's publishing company, through which Charles published all his own songs and encouraged other writers. As a publisher, he was able to share songs around the world through the massive library of material he edited – thirty-five gospel songbooks, eight for Sunday school, seven for male choruses, six specially for ladies, ten for children, nineteen collections of anthems, twenty-three choir cantatas, forty-one Christmas performance pieces, ten cantatas for children and several instruction books for learning and playing music. So many of the most familiar hymns still sung today only became known because of Charles Gabriel's involvement.

This hymn, "I Stand Amazed in the Presence", is becoming popular with a whole new generation of Christians more than a century after it was first published in 1905. It emphasizes the love that Christ showed for us by giving himself as a sacrifice for our sins, and it lists the many ways in which his love for us is expressed. I think, though, it's the catchy chorus that has helped this joyful hymn of praise to become such a favourite. You can't help but have a smile on your face as you stand among a crowd singing, "How marvellous! How wonderful!" It's almost as if we are counting our many blessings throughout the words of each verse.

The pace of life these days is so relentless. For many people, the constant pressure of stress about money, relationships, work, health problems and other frustrations can become an exhausting burden. But this hymn reminds us that Christ took our problems and failings upon himself when he died for us on the cross. In him we find comfort, strength and unconditional love, however wretched or low we are feeling. In this joyful hymn of thanks and wonder, Charles Gabriel reminds us just how marvellous and wonderful it is to have Christ in our hearts.

Lord, in our songs we praise you. In our hearts we worship you. With all we are we magnify your holy name.

AMEN

If Any Little Word of Mine

If any little word of mine
May make a life the brighter,
If any little song of mine
May make a heart the lighter,
God help me speak the little word,
And take my bit of singing,
And drop it in some lonely vale
To set the echoes ringing.

(Robert Walmsley, 1831–1905)

*T*here is some mystery about who exactly wrote these wise words. In Britain we believe they were written by a man born and bred in Manchester, working as a jeweller until the year before he died in his seventies. Robert Walmsley was very involved with the Manchester Sunday School Union, and wrote many songs with children in mind. *Sacred Songs for Children of all Ages* was just one of the forty-four songbooks he published.

In America, almost exactly the same text is attributed to Franklyn E. Belden, who copyrighted his version three years after Robert Walmsley's death – but whereas the hymn was never especially well known here, it remains a favourite in the States. Whoever wrote it, I love these words. In fact, I love *words*, because I think they have power and potential, both for good and bad.

Do you remember that old saying, "Sticks and stones may break my bones, but words can never hurt me"? Well, I know that's not true, because although in time physical wounds might heal, words can wound so deeply that the pain never fades.

I know this sounds quite minor, but I still feel the pain of a comment made years ago, a few months after I'd joined a new school. As I walked past a group of girls I didn't know very well, one of them said, "I can't *stand* that girl..." I felt as if she'd punched me. I know it was a time when I was full of teenage angst, but any sense of self-confidence I had before that moment hit the deck! *Why* didn't they like me? What was it about me that meant they couldn't stand me? Even now, all these years later, I can still feel what I felt then – that I just wanted to run away and hide.

That ongoing hurt comes from a chance comment they probably didn't even know I heard, but when hurtful words are used deliberately by someone who knows you well, then they know the buttons to push to hit those raw nerves inside you with deadly aim. And I think that's why a comment like that can split friends and families for years, because even if what's said has an uncomfortable ring of truth to it, when words are loaded with spite, they hurt.

But equally, when words are filled with love, they too can stay with you forever. I bet we all keep letters and cards from our mums, dads, or from dearly loved friends and relatives, because their words mean so much – words like "I'm proud of you", "Thank you for being all you are", or "No matter what, I will always love you". Words like that are hugs that never leave you. They spur you on to be the best you can be – for those who love you, and for yourself.

Little words can have such power within them – to encourage, reassure, guide and comfort. Just think of the words we hear about in the Bible, especially the ones from Christ himself which reflect his message for us; words like *peace, bless, forgive, love*. The message of those words is universal, whether it's heard by Christians, or people of other faiths or no faith at all. If peace, forgiveness and love are at the heart of all we do, then understanding, tolerance and genuine friendship can follow.

And I have one word of response to that. Amen – or, in other words, so be it!

*Lord, may the words of my mouth and the meditation
of my heart be acceptable in your sight. May we
consider the impact of our words before we open our
mouths to speak, and may we always use the blessing
of speech to praise your holy name.*

AMEN

In Full and Glad Surrender

In full and glad surrender,
I give myself to thee,
Thine utterly and only
And evermore to be.

(Frances Ridley Havergal, 1836–79)

*W*hen Victorian spinster Frances Havergal wrote these words, they plainly came straight from the heart. In spite of the ill health that dogged her for most of her forty-three years, her life was completely dedicated to God, expressed so eloquently in the wealth of hymns and writings that were her legacy – hymns like this one, and the better known "Take My Life and Let it Be", in which her longing to devote her life to the Lord is poured out so personally in every line. Such dedication to faith is something to which many of us aspire, but somehow in modern-day life it can be hard to accomplish alongside all the other calls on our time and energy. But I do still see wholehearted dedication around me – even if not immediately to God!

For example, we have a young man in our family who lives for his football team. He's got the shirt. He's got every photo and write-up he can lay his hands on. He is glued to the telly whenever there's a chance to see them in action, and then he likes nothing more than to talk about every glorious minute of the game to anyone who'll listen. He knows the form, the potential and probably the inside leg measurement of every player on the pitch.

And for someone like me, who's never really got caught up in football mania, I find it quite fascinating that he loves them whatever they do. If they play well, he loves them. If they play badly, he *still* loves them. His dedication is absolute.

But then I suppose that's not unlike the way I feel as a parent. From the moment I first held my son and my daughter in my arms, my dedication to them was absolute too. Oh, I know that over the years they've had their moments of getting things wrong, like all kids – but whatever they've done, however annoyed or embarrassed I might have felt about it, once I'd read them the riot act and the appropriate consequences were put in place, both they and I knew that my disapproval about their behaviour was always within the context of my unconditional love. My absolute dedication to them didn't blind me to their failings, but it meant that the forbidding, disapproving stance I sometimes had to take as a parent stemmed from my loving dedication to them and my hope that they would mature into responsible, caring adults.

I remember coming across a similar dedication some years ago when I had chance to speak at length to a nun who lived in an enclosed order, where they had no television, radio or newspapers. So even though they couldn't possibly have any detailed knowledge of the world's problems, she described the purpose of the sisters as being "a powerhouse of prayer", constantly dedicated to praying for forgiveness for the failings of humanity, and asking, on their behalf, for God's compassion, strength and guidance.

What I remember most is how she spoke of God's absolute dedication to the world and the people he created, and her belief that although he's frustrated by our weakness and failings, he still offers forgiveness and second chances because of his unconditional love for us.

And I think the love I have as a parent, like the love that nun has for the world, and like the absolute devotion of Frances Havergal to her Lord, is simply a reflection of his loving dedication to us.

I owe my life, myself, my all to you, O Lord. You
created me, and I live in the embrace of your love.
May I always cherish that love, in gratitude, in praise
and in dedicated devotion.

AMEN

Jesu, Lover of My Soul

Jesu, lover of my soul,
Let me to thy bosom fly,
While the nearer waters roll,
While the tempest still is high:
Hide me, O my Saviour, hide,
Till the storm of life is past;
Safe into the haven guide,
O receive my soul at last!

(Charles Wesley, 1707–88)

This hymn is such a universal favourite that several quite dramatic stories surround the circumstances in which it was written. One suggestion is that Charles Wesley never forgot the terrible storm he and his brother faced on their trip back from America, and the experience inspired him to write a hymn about the thoughts of a Christian when in deadly danger. Another rather nice but probably fanciful story is that, one summer's day, Charles was standing at an open window when a small bird, chased by a hawk, flew in and buried itself in his coat. Charles was struck by the image, making him think about the soul finding safety in the bosom of God when in desperate need – hence these words!

There is a more positively documented story of how Charles had been preaching in the field of the parish of Killyleagh, in County Down, Ireland, when he was threatened by a group in the crowd who violently disagreed with his views. With the men in hot pursuit, Charles raced off to find safety, finally running into a house where the farmer's wife, Jane Lowrie Moore, told him to hide in the milk house. The angry gang of men were not far behind, and Jane calmed them down by offering them a cold drink, then headed towards the milk house, apparently to get fresh milk. She whispered to Charles to climb out of the back window so he could hide under a hedge that ran along the edge of a small stream. The story goes that, with the cries of his pursuers all around him, Charles sat by the stream and poured out his feelings in the words of this classic hymn.

Whatever the truth of how it was written, what is without doubt is that Charles and John Wesley faced real physical danger on many occasions as they travelled about the country preaching. All too often they were greeted with threats and attack, having to flee for their lives. Just as often, though, people they met on their travels were genuinely interested in what they had to say. On the whole, they were country folk or working people in town communities. At a time when church services were more about doctrine and formality than any recognition of each of us being able to have a personal relationship with a loving God, their message must have been so refreshing and enlightening. The proof of the strength of that message is the existence of the Methodist Church itself, which grew out of a longing for a more personal way of worshipping that appealed to many then, and is the basis of most of our worship today.

There is such wonderful depth of meaning and human emotion laced throughout this text that it's touched countless hearts over the years. All of us face times when we feel overwhelmed, threatened or fearful of what lies ahead of us. It is then that we turn to God with terrible urgency, afraid for our physical or practical welfare, praying for spiritual strength and guidance to help us make the right decision and act in the right way. The words of this hymn provide us with all the prayer we need. In his typically eloquent way, with biblical references in almost every line, Charles Wesley aligns his own humanity with ours. In a way that was never really met with approval by his brother John, Charles makes this hymn intensely poignant and personal – personal to him, and personal to us as, centuries on, we face our own demons and challenges.

Jesu, Lover of My Soul

We are so weak, Father, overwhelmed, uncertain, insecure, frightened for our safety, worried about the future. We ask you to forgive our doubts and open our eyes to your constant grace and presence. We pray that you will draw us to your bosom and hold us there in safety and love.

AMEN

Joshua Fought the Battle of Jericho

Joshua fought the battle of Jericho,
Jericho, Jericho.
Joshua fought the battle of Jericho
And the walls came tumbling down.

You may talk about your king of Gideon,
You may talk about your man of Saul,
But there's none like good old Joshua
And the battle of Jericho.

(Anonymous Afro-American)

*T*here is defiance and deep faith etched into every line of this song, which was born out of the suffering and resilience of Afro-American slaves in the Southern states of America during the early nineteenth century. That story of Joshua leading the Israelites against Canaan seemed to symbolize their own fight to escape from slavery. The song was handed down the generations until it was recorded by huge stars such as Mahalia Jackson and Paul Robeson, who made it known around the world – so famous that it was even recorded by "the King" himself, Elvis Presley!

Elvis could never have imagined being given that title when, in 1954, he walked into Sun Studios in Memphis and recorded "That's All Right". A couple of days later when WHBQ Radio played the track, the switchboard lit up. Elvis gave up his day job as a delivery driver and the music world was changed forever.

A few years back, I spent a week filming with someone who felt the real impact of that change: Pat Boone. Pat was already a huge recording star back in the fifties when he topped the bill one night in Cleveland, Ohio. His supporting act was a newcomer called Elvis Presley, who came on stage swivelling his hips the way only Elvis could. Straight after that, Pat went on in his usual gentlemanly style – smart suit, standing in front of the mike, clicking his fingers – and when he came off, he announced that he would never follow that man on stage again!

But that was actually the start of years of friendship between the two, who shared more than just a talent for show business. They shared their Christian faith, instilled in them as they grew up in the Bible belt of the Southern states of America. It was something they spoke of often

– and they regularly prayed together too, especially on the days when Pat held Christian meetings at his home in Hollywood's Sunset Boulevard, baptizing new Christians in his swimming pool!

But Pat saw less of Elvis as years of worldwide fame, "sex, drugs and rock 'n' roll" took their toll on his friend – until one day they literally bumped into each other at an airport. Elvis hugged Pat with genuine affection, saying several times that he *must* come and see him, because he needed to have a proper talk. They parted company, and a few weeks later Elvis was dead.

Pat was certain that Elvis wanted to reconnect with his faith because he knew the way he was living towards the end of his life wasn't right for his mind, body or soul. He never lost his belief in God. He often read his Bible, and recorded countless gospel songs throughout the length of his career. Once, at a concert, when a group of fans unfurled a banner saying "Elvis is King", he stopped what he was singing, and announced, "There is only one King and that is Jesus Christ."

For years Elvis struggled to connect the two very different lifestyles demanded by fame on the one hand and faith on the other. The trappings of fame were beguiling, disconnecting him from the God he'd always loved, and knew in his heart he needed. Eventually, that cost him his life. "The King" was dead. Let's hope he is now rocking round the throne of the true King, Jesus Christ, *his* Lord.

We all love to be appreciated and praised by others,
Lord. We all want to rise in our chosen field and enjoy
the fruits of our labour and talent. But as success
takes us upwards, we pray we will never forget where
our hearts and souls must be rooted: in you, O King;
in you.

A MEN

Joyful, Joyful, We Adore Thee

Joyful, joyful, we adore thee,
God of glory, Lord of love;
Hearts unfold like flowers before thee,
opening to the sun above.
Melt the clouds of sin and sadness;
drive the dark of doubt away;
Giver of immortal gladness,
fill us with the light of day!

(Henry van Dyke, 1852–1933)

I write this the morning after compèring a wonderful concert in St Alban's Cathedral in Hertfordshire, the spiritual heart of my own diocese. Two hundred and twenty choir members sang this hymn, and that glorious, ancient building seemed to smile along with the thousand-strong audience as the huge vault of its arched ceiling filled with praise and joy. Of course, they were singing it in the style of Whoopi Goldberg in the film *Sister Act*, but as the melody comes courtesy of Beethoven's "Ode to Joy", this only made the whole experience more exhilarating than ever. Surely church buildings were made for this enthusiastic, inclusive, vibrant worship of God!

I imagine that if the writer Henry van Dyke had been with us, he would probably have been on his feet singing along too. I get the impression that even though he was a Presbyterian minister, his personality was anything but stuffy. His easy way with people, combined with his success as an academic, drew him into politics. He had spoken out with his typical sense of balance and fairness in 1898 when America was seeking to annex the Philippines. He told his congregation then:

> *If we enter the course of foreign conquest, the day*
> *is not far distant when we must spend in annual*
> *preparation for wars more than the $180,000,000*
> *that we now spend every year in the education of*
> *our children for peace.*

His talent for balanced argument was noted and later, in 1913, after he'd spent some time lecturing at the University of Paris, he was asked by President Wilson to become America's "man" in the Netherlands and Luxembourg. To take on this role in Europe when the First World War was just a year away needed all his skills of diplomacy and compassion.

It seems that Henry countered that formal side of his life with his romantic, emotional nature, in which he wrote entertaining stories, heart-warming poems and praise-filled hymns. From his pen and from his pulpit, he poured out thought-provoking lines of wisdom and humanity, like:

> *Time is too slow for those who wait, too swift for those who fear, too long for those who grieve, too short for those who rejoice, but for those who love – time is eternity.*

That line of his about time being too short for those who rejoice certainly came to mind as I sang along with "Joyful, Joyful" last night. Years of churchgoing has made me realize just how much music is able to contribute to our worship. We come to God with a wide variety of experiences, concerns and needs, all of which can be reflected in music. It is wonderful to be able to sing enthusiastic hymns of praise, but we also love the quiet, thoughtful hymns that lead us to the Eucharist. In our hymnbooks we find texts that reflect our feelings when we're seeking comfort, encouragement and guidance, which, when sung to just the right piece of music, remain forever in our minds and hearts. No wonder hymns are such a wonderful resource, not just in our worship, but in our lives!

Whoopi Goldberg's toe-tapping version of this hymn may make some people frown with disapproval, but I love the way great words can be given a new lease of life when they are paired with a modern musical treatment, or a fresh approach to the original melody. That's one way in which new generations can discover for themselves the treasure of verses that have been dear to us for years. I'm all for that!

Joyful, joyful, we adore thee, Lord – in our music, in our worship, in our lives! However we are feeling, whatever we are facing, knowing you are present at all times is a source of great joy to us. Hallelujah!

AMEN

Lead Us, Heavenly Father, Lead Us

Lead us, heavenly Father, lead us
o'er the world's tempestuous sea;
guard us, guide us, keep us, feed us,
for we have no help but thee;
yet possessing every blessing,
if our God our Father be.

Saviour, breathe forgiveness o'er us;
all our weakness thou dost know;
thou didst tread this earth before us;
thou didst feel its keenest woe;
yet unfearing, persevering,
to thy passion thou didst go.

(James Edmeston, 1791–1867)

*J*ames Edmeston was an East Londoner through and through. Born and bred in Stepney, he regularly visited the children of the London Orphan Asylum, for whom he wrote a total of 2,000 hymns, one for every

Sunday to be read at family worship. His first collection of hymns, *The Cottage Minstrel*, was published after he'd responded to an advert offering twenty pounds for fifty simple hymns suitable for cottage gatherings. After that he wrote several other collections, including *Infant Breathings* and *Sacred Lyrics*, the book in which this hymn first appeared.

James's dealings with troubled families and orphaned children made him well aware of how "tempestuous" life can be, especially when uncaring behaviour and wrong decisions lead to unhappiness and misunderstanding. In the East End of London, many of his neighbours would have belonged to the large Jewish community who were settled there at the time, and James would have been well aware of Yom Kippur, two days in the year when faithful Jews are asked to look at themselves honestly, and identify ways in which they've not come up to the mark in their service of God or each other.

The truth is, we all know in our heart of hearts that we miss the mark far too often, but most of us simply push away any guilty thoughts and get on with life. The Jewish community, though, aren't allowed to "bury" what they choose not to remember. Yom Kippur forces them to acknowledge where their devotion to God, or their care for others, has been lacking, and in asking for forgiveness, they're able to move on, wiser and hopefully kinder.

But have you noticed how there's nothing more destructive than guilt, resentment or a sense of injustice that lodges like a tight festering knot at the heart of so many people? How many do you know, in your own family perhaps, who've not spoken for years to a sibling or other relative? Long-held grudges, anger at some insult they feel they've suffered, the insistence that, without an apology, they could never consider forgiving the wrong that's been said or done – that can all create a heavy, debilitating load in the pit of the stomach that stops normal life in its tracks. Moreover, that load is a barrier between us and God. How can we even consider saying the Lord's Prayer, with its line asking God to "forgive our sins as we forgive those who sin against us", if the whole idea of forgiveness sticks in the throat?

The sad thing is that it takes so little to start unravelling that knot, because the smallest of words can make a mountain of difference. Words like *sorry, thank you, forgive me, you're right* or *tell me what you think and I'll listen* are immensely difficult to say, and yet have the power to start melting away the burden of resentment and open the path of healing.

So how about we each have our own Yom Kippur? Perhaps we should get round to sending that letter or making that call containing our own important little words because, not just as Christians but as compassionate, mature human beings, we know we should.

Father, help me to be honest with myself, to recognize when I've acted unfairly or spoken thoughtlessly. Purge me of spite, anger and resentment, so that I may hold out the olive branch of caring friendship in a genuine desire not just to feel forgiveness, but to show it to those who've offended me. Make me a channel of your love, Lord, always and to everyone.

AMEN

Little Drops of Water

Little drops of water, little grains of sand,
Make the mighty ocean and the beauteous land.

Little seeds of mercy sewn by youthful hands
Grow to bless the nations far in other lands.

(Julia Carney, 1823–1908)

*C*hildren around the world know this song, which was written by a primary school teacher in Boston, Massachusetts. Julia Carney wrote many pieces especially with children in mind, often using pseudonyms or signing them "anonymous". That was typical of this unassuming lady who, in her later years, was described as an old woman with grey hair who didn't mind one bit about the noise made by the neighbourhood boys as they played ball in the street outside her home. Of all her poems, this one found international fame, quoted by world leaders and cited in a Nobel Prize speech. That was all very grand for Julia, who simply wrote poems she hoped children would love.

For me, that first line about "little drops of water" makes me think about how in the Western world we really do take water for granted. I suppose it's because we live on a group of islands surrounded by sea, and we seem to get more than our fair share of the stuff dropping on us from rain clouds!

But the fact is that half of the people in the world today have a lower level of water and sanitation services than the citizens of Rome had 2,000 years ago. One in six people worldwide don't have access to safe drinking water and, because of that, more than 2 million die every year, most of them children.

That became tragically clear to me some years ago when I travelled with Christian Aid workers to the edge of the Rift Valley in Ethiopia, a country that has suffered dreadfully from drought over the years. Hours of slow, difficult driving cross-country eventually brought us to what seemed to me a bit like a Stone Age settlement. Every day, women and very young children would walk for hours with huge pottery urns on their shoulders to collect water from a tiny lake which was used not just by them, but by their livestock and wild animals too. The water was filthy and infected, and without realizing it, the women were taking back the water they needed to live – but it also caused death. Tragically, those mothers had learned to expect that they might lose their children to cholera or typhoid, or a host of other water-based diseases.

One mum told me that the little boys all had their heads shaved with just a small tuft of hair left at the front so that God had something to hold on to as he pulled them up to heaven.

The solution was really very simple: to intercept the water supply before it reached the lake, so that it could be syphoned off and cleaned up for local communities to drink safely. It didn't take much work. It didn't cost much money. But for those families it was quite simply the difference between life and death.

I believe mothers are the same everywhere, and that those women felt all the grief that any of us would feel if, time after time, we buried our beloved children for lack of something as simple as clean water, a commodity which surely in the twenty-first century should be available for everyone.

But we're very comfortable here. We are so used to having what we need "on tap" that it's easy for us to forget how blessed and fortunate we are. We live in a world of plenty – plenty for us, but what about *them*? Because surely there, but for the grace of God, go we...

Little Drops of Water

Christ, you taught us to love our neighbours, whoever and wherever they are. We live in healthy comfort, while others struggle with life and death issues like starvation, hygiene, healthcare and education. We pray that we will be ever mindful of their needs, creative and practical in the help we offer. Just as you never desert us, may we never desert them.

AMEN

My Hope is Built on Nothing Less

My hope is built on nothing less
Than Jesus' blood and righteousness;
I dare not trust my sweetest frame,
But wholly lean on Jesus' Name.
On Christ, the solid rock, I stand;
All other ground is sinking sand.

(Edward Mote, 1797–1874)

There was very little "hope" that young Edward Mote would ever become a Christian. His parents managed a pub in East London, and often the little boy was left to fend for himself in the street. Once, when asked whether he'd had any religious upbringing, he said, "So ignorant was I that I didn't know there was a God!"

All that had changed by the time he was eighteen, when he chose to be baptized. Ministry wasn't an option he immediately considered, because he was already an apprentice cabinet-maker, a profession he followed for another thirty-seven years. Then, at the age of fifty-five, he finally trained for ordination, becoming the pastor of a Baptist church in Horsham, West Sussex, until he retired. That was twenty-six years later, by which time his congregation loved him so much that they offered him the church building as a gift! He replied, "I do not want the chapel; I only want the pulpit; and when I cease to preach Christ, then turn me out of that!"

Where do you see hope today? In our world where there is so much self-seeking, violence, intolerance, greed and corruption, does hope still exist? While I was thinking about that, my stepdaughter texted that she was sitting in Saturday Morning Cinema with our six-year-old granddaughter who, without warning, said, "I don't know who I am!" A bit taken aback, her mum asked what she meant, and the reply was, "Why was I made and why am I here?"

Wow! Quite something to deal with between the popcorn and hotdogs, but I was glad to hear she'd thought to ask big questions like that; questions we should never stop asking about how each of us fits in the bigger pattern of things.

We all know how we fit within our circle of family and friends, our work and social life, politically or geographically, in age or interest groups. Those are things that can be identified and proved, and it's perfectly possible to live never questioning anything beyond what is known, factual and scientific.

But our granddaughter was asking *why* she was made, *why* she was here, and I believe the answer is far more wonderful than anything science can prove. The vastness and scope of the universe is far beyond our limited understanding, but throughout time, people from all sorts of cultures have instinctively felt that the wonder of life is not just a scientific accident; that there is a creating power with whom they feel a deep longing to connect, soul to soul. An example of that is the way in which the need to pray feels as compelling and natural to many people as it is to sleep, eat or breathe. For me, that power is God, and I believe God is in all of us – and that's not just because I'm a Christian. That's an understanding and experience shared by people of many different faiths and cultures around the world.

How can any of us know all the answers? I certainly don't. But I will never stop searching for the solutions that feel most natural to me. And I am so relieved to know that, in spite of all the technology and material knowledge that surrounds us, young people are still asking those big questions for themselves. Because as long as they are, and as long as they have the chance to hear about God who made and loves each one of us, then there is hope in abundance.

We see your glory, Lord, in everything around us,
but we know that others' eyes are not yet open to

*your truth. We hope and pray that your presence
will be revealed to all, magnificent in your power,
compassionate in your care of every single being into
whom you breathed life.*

AMEN

My Jesus, I Love Thee

My Jesus, I love thee, I know thou art mine;
For thee all the follies of sin I resign.
My gracious Redeemer, my Saviour art thou;
If ever I loved thee, my Jesus, 'tis now.

(William Featherston, 1846–73)

*J*ust look at the dates for William Featherston. He was just twenty-seven when he died, and it's thought that he wrote these words of loving praise to God when he was converted to faith at only sixteen years old. He came from a Methodist family in Montreal, but apparently mailed this text to his aunt in Los Angeles, who saw its worth and set about getting it published. Once the melody had been added to it several years after William's death, it didn't take long before this was a favourite, both in Britain and the States.

There's a lovely story connected to the singing of this hymn which may or may not be true, but it does illustrate the impact of the words. The story goes that, towards the end of the nineteenth century, a talented young actress and singer came across a desperately ill girl whose bed had been moved towards the street door so that she could watch the world outside. The actress stopped to talk to her, and found that there was something about the girl's uncomplaining acceptance of her illness that touched her deeply. She glowed with joy and confidence which, she explained to her new friend, came about because of her deep Christian faith. The actress was so moved that before they parted company she resolved to become a true follower of Christ.

That news didn't go down too well with her father, who was the owner of the theatre company in which she was the popular leading lady. When she told him that she didn't think the life of an actress was consistent with Christian life, he warned her that their business and livelihood would be ruined if she left. Loving her father dearly, she struggled with her disappointment, finally compromising enough to agree to fulfil her role in their performance the following day.

By the time the show was about to start, her father was relieved to see how his daughter was ready as usual for her performance, her declaration of the previous day apparently forgotten. The audience poured in. The curtain rose, and his daughter stepped onto the stage to an enthusiastic round of applause, until something in her expression brought them to curious silence. In the hush, speaking from the heart, she recited the verses of this hymn. It's said that members of the audience were openly weeping as they recognized her sincerity in the beauty of the words – and then, as she walked off stage for the very last time, they applauded her courage and commitment with cheers of admiration.

It took a while for her father to accept her decision, but in the end he agreed with it because, through his daughter, he too eventually came to faith. Together, they went on to use their artistic skills as evangelists, bringing many others to a knowledge of God.

The exact details of that story are lost in the mists of time, but its message of the selfless dedication needed to follow Christ, in spite of any practical difficulties it might cause us, is worth hearing. Our faith does require us to stand up for our principles, and speak out when we see situations that are wrong or unjust. It does ask us to love our neighbours, whoever and wherever they are. Christ tells us that if we tend the sick or visit the prisoner, we are actually serving him. Being a Christian is not always easy but, as that young actress discovered, to live without Christ is no life at all.

Lord, give us the vision to recognize the truth of Christ. Bless us with the courage to follow the path of Christ. Grant us the strength to serve Christ always.

AMEN

New Every Morning is the Love

New every morning is the love
Our wakening and uprising prove;
Through sleep and darkness safely brought,
Restored to life and power and thought.

New mercies each returning day,
Hover around us while we pray;
New perils past, new sins forgiven,
New thoughts of God, new hopes of heaven.

(John Keble, 1792–1866)

In the 1830s, John Keble was one of the leading figures in the Oxford Movement, which wanted to take the Church of England back to its Catholic roots. Unlike others in the group, John never became a Roman Catholic himself, but remained loyal to the church in which he had grown up and was ordained. For ten years around that time he was the Professor of Poetry at Oxford University, and in 1835 he became vicar of the small village of Hursley in Hampshire, where he stayed for thirty years, until his death.

The words of this hymn come from a book of his poems called *The Christian Year*, which sold more than 108,000 copies in forty-three editions – figures which authors would love today, let alone two centuries ago!

For some inexplicable reason, this hymn with its theme of renewal makes me think of car insurance! I've just gone through that convoluted process of renewing the insurance on my car in the way that most of us probably do nowadays, by going on to one of those websites that give you so many choices, it's completely mind-boggling!

You can choose to pay more excess in exchange for lower premiums, or the other way round. You can add courtesy cars or gadget cover or European travel or a breakdown service… the list of options is endless. You're offered pages of different policies, although I guess in the end most of us just go for the cheapest.

So simple "renewal" is probably not the best way to describe what we go through, because every year the whole process is infinitely flexible. We pay our money and make our choice. We might even choose *not* to keep the car and trade it in for a younger model!

A few months back, my husband Richard and I were offered the chance to renew our wedding vows. I thought it was a lovely, romantic idea, but he felt uncomfortable about it. He said that he'd meant all the promises he made during our wedding service, so why would he need to renew them? Didn't it suggest that he might have changed his mind – or perhaps wanted to rewrite the detail to make it a little more flexible and convenient for him now? Wouldn't that be a bit like renewing the policy on the car, or even the car itself? A different colour or style? A more trendy vehicle altogether?

I do see what he means. The really important things in life – what we believe, what we commit to, the people and priorities we feel love and loyalty for – they are the basic truths that define who we are and what matters most to us. And he's right that wedding vows *should* be like that, made sincerely and forever. Inevitably there are challenges to face on the way, great joys along with deep sadness. That's life, constantly changing, which is why, during our marriage services, we pray for the strength to face everything that comes our way together. Our promise made at that time reflects the nature of God himself. He doesn't change in his commitment to us. His promises stand firm, constant and loving.

So I'm glad Richard doesn't want to change or *renew* the promises we made that day – and because he's a bit of a gem really, neither do I!

In our world which is incessantly changing in trend, mood and opinion, we are ever aware of your steadfast faithfulness to us, O Lord. May we reflect that commitment and faithfulness every day in our praise and thanks for your constant, loving care.

AMEN

Now the Day is Over

Now the day is over,
Night is drawing nigh;
Shadows of the evening
Steal across the sky.

Jesus, give the weary
Calm and sweet repose;
With thy tend'rest blessing
May mine eyelids close.

(Sabine Baring-Gould, 1834–1924)

*P*erhaps it was Sabine's rather unusual upbringing that gave him his enthusiasm for life and people. He was named after his great uncle, the Arctic explorer Sir Edward Sabine, and his family's wanderlust meant he spent much of his childhood travelling around Europe, being tutored privately. Money was no problem, because when his father died he inherited the huge family estate in Devon, eventually becoming the parson there as well as the squire.

His life, though, was devoted to ministry, which famously took him as a young curate to Horbury Bridge in the West Riding of Yorkshire. It was there his love for life also turned to romantic love, because he fell for Grace, the daughter of a mill hand, who was then only fourteen. The two courted for four years, until he finally made her his wife. When Grace died, fifteen children and forty-eight years later, Sabine carved on her tombstone the Latin words meaning "Half my Soul".

He had a passion for writing, leaving more than 1,240 publications that we know of today. In particular, his Devon roots gave him a lifelong love of folk songs, and he made use of that simplicity in words and music to write hymns that could be enjoyed by young and old, the literate and the unschooled. There is the delightful tale of him writing his most well-known text, "Onward Christian Soldiers", which he said he "knocked off in about ten minutes" on Whit Saturday afternoon, so that it could be sung by local children during their Whit Tuesday procession through the village.

He lived then in a tiny cottage in which he held a night school downstairs, with a chapel in the bedroom above. Each winter evening, every corner of the house was packed as neighbours poured in to worship, with Sabine balancing on a stool in front of the chimney on which stood a cross and a pair of candlesticks. The crowds also came to learn, because schooling was scarce for most working families then. Children came after a long day's work in the woollen mills, begging him to tell them stories, which he often began with the words every child loves, "Once upon a time..." Sabine knew that stories heard in childhood can stay with us forever, and those Christian truths told in story form on dark winter evenings almost certainly provided the young people with a firm foundation for life. For them – when it seemed only their ability to work had any value, hardship was rife, their rights were non-existent and their opinions irrelevant – these simple Christian principles shaped their actions and reactions, gave them a sense of worth and strength to face the many challenges that came their way.

With those working children in mind, Sabine wrote this evening prayer, "Now the Day Is Over". After the endless hours of their day's work, imagine how soothing and comforting it must have felt to know that they were in God's care, not just overnight, but always.

I remember the lines of prayer my mum said with me every night when I was a child, and I still say them now, decades later. Turning to God in prayer at the end of the day is definitely a recipe for peaceful slumber!

*Lord, through your Son Jesus Christ, you asked that
little children come to you. Help us, as adults, to
show the young people in our care your love through
our own. Give us the words to reassure them of your
constant presence and glory. And however old we are,
may we never stop being your children, called to our
Father in faith and trust.*

AMEN

O Jesus, I Have Promised

O Jesus, I have promised
To serve thee to the end;
Be thou for ever near me,
My Master and my Friend;
I shall not fear the battle
If thou art by my side,
Nor wander from the pathway
If thou wilt be my Guide.

(Ernest Bode, 1816–74)

These words came from a nineteenth-century English minister who loved writing hymns so much that he wrote one for every Sunday and for each festival in the Christian year. This text, though, was very special, because he wrote it in 1866 for the confirmation of his three children – wonderful words of promise as they committed their lives to God.

This brings to mind a remarkable man I met recently who stood by the promise he'd made to God in the most desperate of circumstances. Michael Ho grew up in North Vietnam during the dreadful war there, and experienced first-hand the repercussions that followed once the Communist government finally triumphed in 1975. His brother was taken to a "correction camp" for more than a decade as punishment for siding with the Americans. Christian students like Michael lost their places at university, and there was an atmosphere of fear and hopelessness. More than a million Vietnamese people fled the country, many of them risking their lives in ill-equipped boats at the mercy of the South China seas in search of freedom. It's estimated that more than 400,000 Boat People perished.

Michael's family paid a high price for his place on a boat. It was designed for thirty people, but it set sail under cover of darkness with seventy-seven people on board, all crammed in the hold for two days for fear of being seen by the authorities as they sailed along the coast. Food and water rations had gone by day two, and on day three they ran out of fuel, leaving them floating helplessly, tossed in unsettled seas, growing weaker and more desperate.

On the seventeenth day, a young woman gave birth prematurely. Michael was one of the only people with enough strength to help her, and the love and happiness he saw as the mother held her son prompted him to fall to his knees, pleading with God, "How can you bring such a beautiful child into the world when we have no food and no hope?" And he went on to promise that if God saved this little boy, Michael would devote his life to him.

An hour later, a British cargo ship, the *Ben Dearg*, loomed onto the horizon. Other ships had simply passed them by, but this one came nearer, circling their boat until it finally dropped anchor beside them. The captain realized he didn't have room for seventy-seven new passengers, but after one look at their desperate state, he ordered them aboard. Several days later, they reached the safety of Singapore, where most of the group decided to travel onward to America or Australia. Touched by the unquestioning kindness of the British crew, Michael decided to head for Britain. Within months of arriving, having been met by equal kindness in the UK, he committed himself to becoming a Catholic priest, keeping his promise to devote his life to God's service.

Michael recently celebrated thirty years of ministry, and I had the delightful privilege a few months back of being with him when *Songs of Praise* tracked down the second mate from the *Ben Dearg*, the man who had rescued that young mother from their little boat. Michael was able to tell him that the baby boy born the day they'd met was now a healthy, settled father himself! There were many tears at that meeting – tears of relief, gratitude and praise to God for saving not just Michael's life, but so many other Vietnamese people at their time of despair.

Faithful Father, your promise to us is constant and enduring. Our faith, though, can be fickle and often forgotten as we become absorbed in our own lives. We pray for forgiveness, and for strength in our resolve to put you at the centre of everything we do.

AMEN

O Little Town of Bethlehem

O little town of Bethlehem,
How still we see thee lie!
Above thy deep and dreamless sleep
The silent stars go by.
Yet in thy dark streets shineth
The everlasting light;
The hopes and fears of all the years
Are met in thee tonight.

(Phillips Brooks, 1835–93)

This dearly loved Christmas carol was written by an American Episcopal priest, rector of Trinity Church in Boston. In 1865, he fulfilled his wish to visit the Holy Land, travelling across Palestine in time to arrive in Bethlehem on Christmas Eve. He was deeply moved by the experience, and carried the memory with him for three years before writing these words for the children of the Sunday school at his church. His organist, Lewis Redner, added the tune most usually sung across the

States, although in Britain it was the great Ralph Vaughan Williams who collected a folk ballad from a man living in Forest Green, Surrey, and his adaptation of that melody has been associated with the carol ever since.

Just like Phillips Brooks, I too had a very moving experience in Bethlehem not long ago. I was there as one of the leaders on a pilgrimage of about 150 people, visiting places with familiar names from our Bibles. It's always a very emotional experience – and an exhausting one too, as there are so many sites to see in a short space of time, and no pilgrim wants to miss out on any of them.

There were about fifty of us travelling on our coach, and I soon became aware of an undercurrent of exasperation among some of the group about a delightful but quite elderly lady, Phyllis. She was really struggling to keep up with the rest of us, to the extent that some were concerned she was holding up the whole party. It was clear, though, that she just couldn't walk any faster, for the simple reason that she was wearing the most inappropriate shoes: huge open-toed leather flip-flops that seemed to be several sizes too big for her. No wonder she needed to walk slowly over the uneven surfaces in the ancient places we were visiting!

Finally, the inevitable happened. She lost her footing and took a nasty tumble, which left her badly shaken rather than hurt. For the rest of the afternoon,

I kept her company as we walked around, leaving the others in the group to make their visits more speedily without us. As we walked, she told me her story. This pilgrimage was something she'd dreamed of doing for years, and when she finally booked it, she'd bought a ticket not just for herself, but also for her son, because they really wanted to share the experience together. Tragically, soon after that he developed a severe form of cancer, and by the time the trip came around, he was far too ill to travel. So she decided to take him with her by wearing his shoes, so that she could walk in the footsteps of Christ for him.

What faith! What love! And what echoes of that other young mother in Bethlehem 2,000 years ago! She too gave birth to a son she loved; taught and cared for him as he grew; felt pride in his achievements as a young man – when all the time she had a sense of foreboding that she would one day watch him die.

Both these mothers had such love and faith, and for Mary that was rewarded when, as Christians believe, her son rose from the dead to fulfil God's will.

And when Phyllis walked in Christ's footsteps in her own son's shoes, she was accepting God's will too, whatever that might be. Now that's a mother's love for you…

Sometimes, Lord, we judge others too quickly, and our treatment of them is ill-informed and insensitive. We pray for the wisdom and care to get to know the people we meet, so that we can understand their concerns, and support them in their need. Strengthen our faith, Father. Help us to walk in the footsteps of Christ in our own lives.

AMEN

O Worship the King

O worship the King, all-glorious above;
O gratefully sing his power and his love;
Our shield and defender, the Ancient of Days,
Pavilioned in splendour and girded with praise.

Thy bountiful care what tongue can recite?
It breathes in the air, it shines in the light;
It streams from the hills, it descends to the plain,
And sweetly distils in the dew and the rain.

(Sir Robert Grant, 1779–1838)

Robert Grant was a Scottish Anglican, a deeply devout evangelical Christian who was born into high political life in India, where his father was a director of the East India Company. Later, Robert became a member of the British parliament from Scotland, and eventually was appointed Governor of Bombay. When he died there, the people of India chose to honour him by establishing a medical college in his name.

This hymn was inspired by a sixteenth-century hymn by William Kethe which, in turn, was based on Psalm 104. It is rich with words of gratitude, a prayer of thankfulness to God.

I have to say that I don't think we say thank you anywhere near enough these days. I'm old-fashioned enough to notice the fact that children now rarely send thank-you letters to the people who have lovingly chosen and prepared presents for them for birthdays and Christmas. It's not that thanks are needed, but a little message of appreciation means a lot.

But the biggest thank you of all must surely be due not for what we're *given*, but for what we already *are* – all the talents, physical traits and personality that make us unique individuals; qualities that were attributed to us before we were even born. People of faith consider those qualities as God-given, a mixture of blessings and limitations that shape our actions and reactions throughout our whole lives. The range can be so varied: some of us are artistic; some are academic, good with words or figures; some are physically very strong, and skilled with our hands; others are empathetic and caring, able to teach, guide and support those who are struggling with their own challenges.

The important thing is not just to be grateful for the gifts we've been given, but to recognize we were given them for a purpose – to help ourselves, but also to make life easier for others.

I remember Cliff Richard telling me on *Songs of Praise* years ago how, when he was in his early twenties, topping the charts at the height of his career, he was asked to become a patron of the newly formed Christian relief agency, Tearfund. His first job was to visit a very impoverished area of India, where the human hardship and suffering he saw hit him hard. He was watching a nurse give life-saving medication to a baby when he announced that, challenged by what he'd seen, he couldn't possibly go back to the glittering, superficial life of a popstar. He was going to give it all up to become a volunteer in the Third World.

The nurse looked at him scathingly. "Can you give an injection?" she asked.

"No," he said.

"Then leave this work to the people who are trained to do it. You have other talents, which have made you a worldwide name. Use your fame to tell the world what's happening here. You do what *you* can, so *we* can be supported to do our work here."

Thank God for Cliff's talents, which have allowed him to do his best to get that message out over the years, and thank God for his gifts to each and every one of us! Let's make sure that we use those talents not just for our own fulfilment, but for the benefit of others who need the help God knows we are equipped to give.

*Thank you, Lord, for all we are. Help us to recognize
the richness of your gifts to us, and use those gifts
wisely and with compassion.*

AMEN

Rock of Ages

Rock of ages, cleft for me,
Let me hide myself in thee,
Let the water and the blood,
From thy wounded side which flowed,
Be of sin the double cure,
Save from wrath and make me pure.

(Augustus Toplady, 1740–78)

If you're going to be a hymn-writer, you've got to have a name to match the task – and names don't come much grander and more impressive than this one! Augustus had his father, Major Richard Toplady, to thank for his memorable surname, although he probably remembered little else of the soldier who died in service while his son was still a toddler. His mother was left comfortably well-off, able to send Augustus to the prestigious Westminster School, and later to Trinity College in Dublin. It was there, at the age of sixteen, having gone along to an evangelical gathering in what he described as "an obscure part of Ireland, midst a handful of people met together in a barn", that "by the ministry of one who could hardly spell his own name" he felt a deep calling not just to faith, but to ordination.

For a while he was attracted to the ministry of his contemporaries John and Charles Wesley, but in time he became increasingly outspoken in his criticism of the Methodist ethos, both from his Anglican pulpit and in *The Gospel Magazine*, for which he often wrote. In the article in which "Rock of Ages" first appeared, he revealed a great deal about his own philosophy. He said he'd calculated that the average person committed 2,522,880,000 sins during their lifetime, and that, just as England would never be able to repay the country's national debt, so none of us will ever be able to satisfy our eternal debt to God through our own meagre efforts! Ending his article with the verses of "Rock of Ages", Augustus described the text as "a living and dying prayer for the holiest believer in the world"!

Well, did that huge number knock you sideways, as it did me? I mean, just how big has a sin got to be before it counts? If you're not doing anything wrong, but not actually doing anything right either, is that a sin? Is a white lie a sin, even though you're bending the truth a little to save another's feelings? Or if, during a busy day, you hurry past your neighbour's door even though you know she's not able to get out much, and it would really cheer her up if you popped in to say hello? Is it a sin if you've had a lovely evening out on Saturday and can't manage to open your eyes in time for church on Sunday morning? Or if you notice who's calling your phone, then pretend you didn't hear it ring? Or, if someone asks you how much you weigh, is it a sin if you round it down half a stone – just as you might knock off a year or two if someone asks how old you are? Have you ever lost something, then kept quiet when someone else was blamed? Or made an accusation that hurt and humiliated another person's feelings, only to realize later that you didn't check your facts and you were wrong? Our daily lives are a long succession of small decisions, actions and reactions which can be judged by the eye of the beholder. It does us no harm, perhaps during our prayers at the end of each day, to think back on how we might have been kinder, worked harder or cared more. I think God knows us and understands our weakness, but his hope for us is that we recognize our failings and genuinely try to do better. Do you think there's any chance we could get that huge total of our own sins down a billion or so?

God of love, understanding and forgiveness, help us
to be more like you. You blessed us with eyes to see,
hands to work, lips to smile and a heart to care. May
we use all those blessings wisely and with compassion.

AMEN

Shall We Gather at the River?

Shall we gather at the river,
Where bright angel feet have trod;
With its crystal tide forever
Flowing by the throne of God?

Yes, we'll gather at the river,
The beautiful, the beautiful river;
Gather with the saints at the river
That flows by the throne of God.

(Robert Lowry, 1826–99)

*H*ow many cowboy films can you think of that feature this song? Quite a few directed by John Ford, because he always said he loved it. From John Wayne classics like *Stagecoach*, right up to Clint Eastwood in *Hang 'Em High*, this hymn was the unforgettable star of many a Western movie.

Robert Lowry, who wrote both the words and music, may have lived during the cowboy era, but his lifestyle couldn't have been more different. Having dedicated his life to ministry in his early twenties, he became a humorous and entertaining preacher, weaving facts and information into worship and praise. Playing a variety of musical instruments had come easily to him since childhood, and it wasn't long before he was combining his flowing way with words and his skill as a musician to produce hundreds of gospel songs.

One sultry afternoon in 1864, he was sitting at his desk in Elliott Place, Brooklyn, when the idea for this hymn came to him. At the time, an epidemic was sweeping through the city, bringing mourning to almost every household. Struggling to deal with his own grief as he heard of the death of yet another friend, Robert became obsessed with words from the first verse of Revelation chapter 22:

> *Then the angel showed me the river of the water*
> *of life, as clear as crystal, flowing from the throne*
> *of God and of the Lamb down the middle of the*
> *great street of the city.*

"Shall we meet again?" Robert pondered. "We are parting at the river of death. Shall we meet at the river of life?" Later, in his own words, he described how the song formed in his mind:

> *Seating myself at the organ simply to give vent*
> *to the pent-up emotions of the heart, the words*
> *and music of the hymn began to flow out, as if by*
> *inspiration.*

The hymn soon became a favourite in Sunday schools throughout New York, and the following year on Children's Day 40,000 youngsters from the city's churches sang it together. Sometime later, Robert was invited to a meeting at the Old Bailey in London, to join a gathering of Sunday school teachers from around the world. He sat alone at the back, and was about to leave when the chairman announced that the author of "Shall We Gather at the River?" was there. The standing ovation he received from church leaders from all over Europe, Asia and the States brought home to him how his hymn, so quickly and spontaneously written, had struck a chord with Christians from all corners of the globe.

Robert Lowry had the knack of phrasing complex spiritual truths very simply, often with the help of an image that made them easy to visualize. By basing his words on the image of the river of life, he created a hymn that brings confidence and reassurance to those weighed down by the hard knocks of everyday living.

Down the centuries there have been countless learned theologians who've had very definite views on the rights and wrongs of interpreting the words of the Bible, and yet sometimes it's the straightforward thought, the simple image, the conversational phrase, that brings the point home to us most vividly, touching our imagination, our logic and our hearts in the most personal way. To hear a description of the immense majesty and wonder of God in a down-to-earth way makes the Christian message more accessible and real for us – simple language for simple truths.

Lord, help us to appreciate the magnitude of your greatness and strength as well as the intimate comfort of your presence and love. And bless those who have the skill to bring your glorious truths to the level of our understanding in a way that reveals and inspires.

AMEN

Teach Me, My God and King

Teach me, my God and King,
In all things thee to see,
And what I do in anything
To do it as for thee.

(George Herbert, 1593–1633)

*G*eorge Herbert could have risen to high political office, but instead chose the life of a country clergyman. Growing up in an aristocratic family, he counted John Donne as a friend, became a Member of Parliament and even attracted the admiring notice of King James I. His health was never strong, though, and eventually the quieter country life gave him the peace he needed not only to explore his faith, but to write some of the most beautiful poetry in the English language. His own opinion of his work was typically humble, and a few weeks before his death, when he gave a book of verse to his close friend, he wrote that "he shall find in it a picture of the many spiritual conflicts that have passed betwixt

God and my soul". That challenging relationship comes to mind in the first verse of this hymn, in which George asks his God to teach him what he needs to know.

Now, any of us who are parents know how difficult it is to teach someone else, especially when it's our children. It's always tempting to want to pass on the wisdom of our own experience, even making the terrible mistake of starting with that dreaded line, "When I was your age..." They instantly glaze over with the look that says, "You were *never* my age!"

But although it's true that the feelings are probably much the same even though their situation and circumstances nowadays are quite different from ours, life has taught us so many lessons, one of which is that you never learn from other people's experience, only from your own. So we have to watch from the sidelines as a younger generation reinvents the wheel, then resist the urge to say "I told you so!" when the wheel falls off, as we knew it would!

And we have to hope that our parenting skills and guidance will help them to realize the truths we've already learned. We want them to understand that every action has a consequence, and that the more you work, the more you'll achieve. We hope they'll realize that if they treat others with respect and friendship, they are likely to be shown the same in return. And when they moan that they want their lives to be different, we long for them to realize that the only way in which change will come about is if they do something positive themselves to make that change happen.

But more than that, we hope our children come to realize that, as human beings, we have a natural longing in three particular ways. Our bodies hunger for health and our minds thirst for knowledge, two longings we recognize with an instant response. But that leaves our souls, and the acknowledgment of the craving within each of us to connect in a deeply personal way with the God who created and loves us. How do we explain to others what we've experienced ourselves – the comfort, strength and guidance we've found in faith, and the richness and power of prayer throughout our lives?

Well, in truth, finding faith is a deeply personal experience for each one of us, often starting with a small step of recognition which can lead to a blessed wealth of perception and understanding. And of all life's lessons, that's the one I most hope my children will come to discover for themselves.

Father God, we long to learn your will for us, and
we pray for wisdom and guidance as we try to teach
those lessons to the next generation. Grant us the
patience, the insight and the sensitivity to reveal to
them a glimpse of the greatness we see in you.

AMEN

The Battle Hymn of the Republic

*Mine eyes have seen the glory of the coming of
the Lord;*
*He is trampling out the vintage where the grapes
of wrath are stored;*
*He hath loosed the fateful lightning of his terrible
swift sword:*
His truth is marching on.
Glory, glory hallelujah! Glory, glory hallelujah!
Glory, glory hallelujah!
His truth is marching on.

(Julia Ward Howe, 1819–1910)

*J*ust after Winston Churchill's funeral in 1965, his wartime co-leader and friend General Eisenhower explained that the most moving part of the funeral for him was when this hymn was sung. He knew it to be one of Churchill's favourites because he had learned it in childhood from his American mother. A paraphrase of what Eisenhower said is this:

We all know the first verse, "Mine eyes have seen the glory" – but do you know the third verse? Because there I was seated with heads of state from France, the Netherlands, Norway and Belgium, all nations whose freedom had been redeemed by the warrior who lay in state only yards before us. And I could see feelings of gratitude and reverence mist their eyes, as they did my own as we sang these words: "He sounded forth the trumpet that shall never call retreat..."

Those tears were in memory of Churchill's dogged determination throughout the darkest hours of the war, when the march of Hitler and the Nazis across Europe seemed impossible to overcome. His vision and resilience were nothing less than inspirational, filling the Allies' forces with confidence and conviction. Churchill never sounded retreat – quite the opposite. "Never! Never! Never!" was his response to that!

This hymn which inspired Churchill and countless other fighting men was surprisingly written by a woman, Julia Ward Howe, who was born into an affluent family in New York City in 1819. As befitted her society upbringing, she married "well" in 1843 to a man eighteen years older than her. Samuel Howe was a domineering husband who immediately limited his wife's activities, taking control of her money, which he mismanaged so badly he almost ruined them. When he eventually died in 1876, she commented, "Start my new life today!"

She'd always loved writing, and dedicated that skill to promoting causes dear to her heart. On one occasion when she visited a Union army camp, she heard soldiers singing "John Brown's Body", a song honouring the prominent abolitionist who'd been hanged for treason. She loved the melody, but despised the words, so stayed up way into the night scribbling down these verses. When she later offered her poem to a local magazine, she was delighted to be paid five dollars!

The new song quickly spread in popularity throughout the Union army and, before long, across the nation. Although Julia had taken her inspiration from passages in the book of Revelation, the images she conjured up by using words like "wrath", "judgment", "sword" and "trumpet" spoke loudly not just to soldiers in battle, but also to statesmen in leadership, and ordinary people as they fought to make the most of their lives.

Julia faced her own battles as a downtrodden, patronized wife. Then, within the male-dominated society of that time when the opinions of women were considered to be of little importance, she struggled to ensure her voice was heard and her views were valued. She spoke up for the rights of women. She stood up for the abolition of slavery and campaigned tirelessly for education reform and learning opportunities available for all. She knew from personal experience how demoralizing it was to be belittled and unappreciated in a way that undermines confidence and any sense of worth. But, as a lifelong Christian, she believed that she was unique and valued, blessed and loved unconditionally by God.

Lord, when we are dismissed as unimportant, our views irrelevant, our feelings unnoticed, it makes us feel worthless. But each one of us is precious in your sight. Just as you love us, you ask us to love each other. May we always be aware of the feelings and needs of others, and treat all with the respect and care they deserve.

AMEN

The God of Abraham Praise

The God of Abraham praise, who reigns
enthroned above
Ancient of everlasting days and God of love:
Jehovah, great I AM, by earth and heaven
confessed;
I bow and bless the sacred name for ever blessed.

(Thomas Olivers, 1725–99)

The title of this hymn, "The God of Abraham Praise", is based on a verse from the book of Exodus: "I am the God of thy Father, the God of Abraham."

I doubt that the Welsh author Thomas Olivers would have had an interest in anyone's God when he was growing up in Tregynon in Montgomeryshire. His father died three years after he was born, followed by his mother a year later, so he was brought up first by an elderly uncle, then a succession of other relatives, and this resulted in very little education or discipline. He managed to get an apprenticeship with a shoemaker but, as he later said himself, he was lazy and irresponsible, eventually leaving home to travel wherever his basic skills as a cobbler might earn him a little money.

On one occasion, he was in Bristol when, by chance, he heard George Whitefield, the leading Methodist preacher, speaking. When George said, "Is this not a brand plucked from the fire?" (from Zechariah 3:2) the young man felt sure the sermon was aimed directly at him. That was the start of Thomas's twenty-five years of ministry, especially after John Wesley himself spotted the young man's talent as a preacher, and encouraged him to take the Christian message to the far ends of the country – Dundee at one time, Cornwall another. There's a story that Thomas set out on foot, as usual, to Cornwall, but only got as far as Tiverton in Devon before his feet were killing him. The solution was to spend five pounds on a colt that became his constant companion over years of travelling and preaching.

In 1770, Thomas was staying with the hymn-writer John Bakewell in London, when he visited a service in a synagogue. There he heard a Jewish cantor known as Leoni singing the Yigdal, a Hebrew doxology listing the thirteen articles of the Jewish Creed which is usually sung at the close of divine service on the eve of the Sabbath. The tune was so ancient that, as a Jew, Christ may well have sung this himself. Thomas was so moved by the song's beauty that he resolved to translate the words into

English and paraphrase their meaning with a Christian focus, to fit the tune which is still known as "Leoni" today.

The comment was once made about this hymn that "there is not in our language a lyric of more majestic style, more elevated thought, or more glorious imagery". For me, its real strength and beauty lie in the way in which it draws on the rich traditions and depth of the Hebrew faith to inform and enhance our understanding of Christ himself, who was born, lived and died as a Jew.

Today, when there is so much division between different religions, it's all too easy to overlook how much we have in common. The square mile around the old temple in Jerusalem is sacred to all three of the great world faiths of Judaism, Islam and Christianity, rooted in the history they share from the Old Testament. As Jonathan Sachs, until recently the Chief Rabbi of Great Britain, said to me, "There is only one God, but he speaks many different languages."

Lord, the melody and meaning of this hymn would have been a familiar part of Christ's own worship. We celebrate all we share with others who know you as Lord. Through Christ, your Son, we pray for all who truly love you.

AMEN

Through All the Changing Scenes of Life

Through all the changing scenes of life,
In trouble and in joy,
The praises of my God shall still
My heart and tongue employ.
Of his deliverance I will boast,
Till all that are distressed
From my example courage take
And soothe their griefs to rest.

(Nahum Tate, 1652–1715)

When it comes to the ups and downs of life, Nahum Tate certainly had more than his share of both. He was born in Dublin, but took himself to London as a young man. He aspired to be a poet, but that didn't pay the rent, so he took a day job translating French and Latin texts for publishers. In his spare time, he wrote plays of his own or altered the works of established playwrights like Shakespeare. He rewrote the great tragedy of *King Lear* to give it a happy ending, with Cordelia escaping death to marry Edgar! Although he lived most of his life in poverty, he did eventually become Poet Laureate, but his love of drink got the better of him, and he died in a debtors' refuge within the precincts of the Royal Mint.

Looking back over my own life, I recognize, as Nahum plainly did, that I have been through many different stages of experience which have helped to mature my thinking. For example, many years ago I used to present the live television evening news programme for the East of England. One Christmas, all the female presenters on the programme received a joint greetings card from a man serving a long prison sentence in the area. He wrote something about each of us:

> *Christine – beautiful, glamorous*

> *Helen – gorgeous, desirable*

And right at the bottom:

> *Pam Rhodes – girl next door, nice smile, will*
> *make a good wife and mother*

Well, this was a man who presumably hadn't seen women for years, and even for him I didn't merit pin-up status! I remember being quite put out at the time, but turn the clock on thirty or more years and I have to say I've really grown to appreciate the compliment he paid me.

I suppose, when we're young, how we look really matters, but nowadays I'm free of that worry because my priorities have become very different. Love, kindness, loyalty, commitment, integrity – they're the qualities I really value in everyone, but mostly in myself: in my family life as a wife and mum (and he was quite right, I *do* love those roles!); in work, in friendships and in my hopes for what lies ahead.

Since I was a small child, I've learned about those qualities from the very best of teachers, Christ himself, who spent so much of his time on earth giving guidelines about how people have to be if they want to live in harmony with those around them. I'm full of good intentions, like everyone else I expect, and I know I often get things wrong by not giving the needs of others enough consideration. But I've found a good question to ask myself when I'm wondering if I'm guilty of that: "What would Christ do?" I usually find the answer is easy. What's hard is living up to the challenge it presents. But then challenge creates character! I can look back now and see that it's the toughest times I've been through that have pushed me to discover what I'm really made of, what I'm capable of being – and what truly matters to me now.

So I really don't mind being the lady next door

with a nice smile who's a good wife and mother – or the character that's etched all over my face, because I know those lines round my eyes come from years of smiling. But then, being blessed in so many ways, I do have a lot to smile about.

We live to learn. From what we learn, we have the choice to live more considerately, kindly and usefully. Dear Lord, help us to learn the most valuable lessons in life by keeping the commandments Christ gave us, and by caring for others as we would wish to be treated ourselves.

AMEN

We Plough the Fields, and Scatter

We plough the fields, and scatter
The good seed on the land,
But it is fed and watered
By God's almighty hand;
He sends the snow in winter,
The warmth to swell the grain,
The breezes and the sunshine,
And soft refreshing rain:

All good gifts around us
Are sent from heaven above;
Then thank the Lord, O thank the Lord,
For all his love.

(Matthias Claudius, 1740–1815; tr. Jane Campbell, 1817–78)

*H*arvest just wouldn't be the same without the chance to sing this hymn so associated with the traditional festivals held by every church in autumn to give thanks to God for the harvest bounty of yet another year. Nowadays, supermarkets with their packaged and frozen foods detach us from the land and its gifts to us, so it's important and heart-warming each year to recognize that however sophisticated farming has become, at the heart of all we eat and enjoy is God's creation.

This hymn was originally written by Matthias Claudius, a newspaper journalist in Germany, to the melody of an old peasants' song, and it was translated into English by a vicar's daughter, Jane Montgomery Campbell, for a hymnbook she was compiling for children.

And thinking of children, it occurred to me that it's not only plants that are God's creation for which we are required to be loving stewards, responsible for their nurture and development. Above all, our children are the harvest of our own lives and, as parents, we want them to achieve their full potential as healthy, fulfilled and contented adults. Mind you, when they burst into our world as squawking, terrifying, newborn babies, they come with fewer instructions than you'd find on a packet of garden seeds!

The practical nuts and bolts of bringing up children are pretty obvious, but I reckon we could all add our own not-so-obvious suggestions to the list – nuggets of good advice we've gleaned on the way which could be the magic additives to help our "seedlings" grow.

Top of my list is *love*, which is surely the best compost in which confident, compassionate youngsters flourish. And this may be an old-fashioned thought, but I reckon one of the greatest gifts parents can give their children is simply to love each other. Nowadays, families can be so fractured, and children confused and wounded when the adults in their lives aren't able to give an example of loving commitment to one another.

And what could feel more loving to a child than our *time* spent with them? Children long for our interest and attention. If we make time for them now, they'll have time for us in the future.

How about every now and then letting them overhear you say something really nice about them? Appreciation is so much more encouraging than criticism. Let them know how much you value them, and watch their confidence grow as they come into the full bloom of their potential.

Lastly, when children grow up in a faithful household, where God is acknowledged and there's an acceptance that we should treat others as we hope to be treated ourselves, that's not just the basis for well-rounded individuals, but for contented families and caring communities too. A recognition that there is a power beyond our own gives us the reassurance and strength we need to be everything God intends us to be.

The nature of our children may come from God, but their nurture is our responsibility. And as any gardener or farmer knows, if we get the growing conditions right, our "little petals" will flourish to become blooming marvellous!

Lord of creation, may we value the blessing of all your many gifts. In particular, we give our heartfelt thanks for our children – and the wonderful mix of joy, challenge, laughter, worry and love they bring to our lives. May we always protect, guide and cherish them as a reflection, dear Father, of your love for us.

AMEN

Ye Holy Angels Bright

Ye holy angels bright,
who wait at God's right hand,
or through the realms of light
fly at your Lord's command,
assist our song,
for else the theme
too high doth seem
for mortal tongue.

(Richard Baxter, 1615–91)

By the time Richard Baxter wrote this hymn, he was a minister with a chequered past. It was at a time in English history when it was unwise to challenge the religious authorities at the heart of government, which was difficult for a man full of questions and a passion to find the truth of Christ's sacrifice and our relationship with God.

He'd served as one of Oliver Cromwell's chaplains during the English Civil War, then later became chaplain to Charles II, who offered him the role of Bishop of Hereford. When he turned that down because, among other things, he couldn't accept the Book of Common Prayer, doors closed against him, and he left the Church of England to become a nonconformist minister. From the early 1660s he faced constant persecution of one kind or another, until in 1680, when he was grieving the loss of his wife and frail from ill-health, his books were seized and he was dragged three times to the court-house without any real cause. Most frightening of all, in May 1685 he was called before the notorious Chief Justice, the dreaded Judge Jeffreys, charged with libelling the church in his many books and articles. The judge sentenced him to stay in prison for up to seven years until a heavy fine was paid, and even proposed that the seventy-year-old man should be whipped behind a cart, which thankfully didn't happen. In fact, after eighteen months, Richard was released from prison because the government was growing increasingly aware of how influential his writings had become.

Through all the difficulty, as we see in this hymn, Richard Baxter always had an image of heaven, where angels surround God's glorious throne. While Christians are used to angels being mentioned throughout the Bible, it's harder to imagine that they are still at work for us today. During my time on *Songs of Praise* I have met several very down-to-earth people who've shared with me their totally unexpected experience of meeting what they came to believe was an angelic presence. Sometimes they described someone apparently human who appeared at a moment of great stress or danger, caring, calming, saving life and limb. Others described traditional angelic figures that they'd seen clearly beside a loved one who was dying. One lady told me how just such a figure appeared in her living room when she was alone with three small children while a terrifying riot was raging on the estate where they lived. Another man described, with great emotion, how four angelic figures had moved to and fro along the length of his body as he lay in bed with chronic back pain, and that since that time he'd not suffered any further disability.

Christians in the twenty-first century seem wary of putting too much store by the possibility of angels making appearances among our own communities. Many are equally careful about how they view reports of physical healing as a result of prayer. However, others feel that if we are told in the Bible of angels and acts of healing as an integral part of Christ's own ministry on earth, then why should they not continue to be part of God's love for us now?

Limited by our own meagre humanity, there is so much we don't and can't possibly know about the glory of God and the extent of his gifts to us. We simply recognize that his power is infinite and that anything is possible through him, even if we find it hard to believe in this day and age. Let go, let God. His will be done.

Father, open our minds to all that you are. Grant us the vision and wisdom to recognize your hand in all things, and to trust in your unending love for us.

AMEN

Don't miss…

Love So Amazing

PAM RHODES
Love So Amazing
40 Reflections on my favourite hymns

"Truly inspiring, reminding us of God's faithfulness, presence and grace in our daily lives."

Dave Bilbrough, songwriter and contemporary worship leader

Pam Rhodes brings together reflections on some of her favourite hymns. Drawing on her experience of presenting *Songs of Praise* and sharing the stories of hymn writers past and present, she helps us to make use of their words in expressing our joys and sorrows to God, and in finding hope and inspiration. Whatever our circumstances, these hymns turn us again to the God who created, knows and sustains us with that "love so amazing" described in the immortal words of hymn writer Isaac Watts.

"Pam brings to the page a warmth and freshness, enabling these hymns to lift our hearts to God and point us again to Jesus."
Bishop Timothy Dudley-Smith, hymnwriter

"Pam Rhodes brings a warm personal touch to the telling of some great stories about the greatest hymns."
Sally Magnusson, journalist, broadcaster, and writer

ISBN: 978-0-85721-570-3 | e-ISBN: 978-0-85721-571-0

Fiction from Pam Rhodes:

FISHER *of* MEN

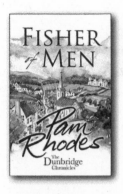

*"Pam's book is a great read!
It's a tale of real people who laugh,
have fun and love life. I commend it
warmly."*

George Carey, former Archbishop
of Canterbury

*Neil Fisher's first trip to Dunbridge was not a success. Having
inadvertently locked himself in St Stephen's church for hours (and
succumbing to the communion wine and wafers for dinner) it seemed
miraculous they gave him the curate's job!*

On arrival in the small town of Dunbridge it quickly
becomes clear that life is not going to be tranquil for the
eligible new bachelor, as four formidable women are
determined to make their presence felt.

There is his mother, Iris, still questioning his choice of
career; his rector, the no-nonsense Margaret, who is not one
for taking prisoners; Claire, his new neighbour, whom he's
already managed to offend. And then there is Wendy, the
beautiful leading light of the church music group, who has
her own plans for Neil...

It can only end in trouble.

ISBN: 978-1-78264-000-4 | e-ISBN: 978-1-78264-001-1

WITH HEARTS AND HYMNS AND VOICES

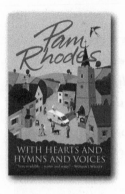

"Very moving, very powerful intimate moments... I really did enjoy it."

Lynn Parsons, BBC Radio 2

When the BBC *Songs of Praise* team decides to broadcast a Palm Sunday service from a small idyllic Suffolk village, not everyone is happy.

The vicar, Clive, is amiably absent-minded, but his practical wife Helen gets on well with the television team – perhaps a little too well, where the charming, enigmatic Michael is concerned. Charles, the Parish Council chairman, is deeply opposed and resents the enthusiasm of other villagers – including his wife Betty. As the outside broadcast vehicles roll in, the emotional temperature rises...

"Very readable... Warm and witty."
Woman's Weekly

"A gripping story which touches some very basic emotions... Captures wonderfully the two extremes of village life... This is very powerful stuff."
Barbara Erskine

ISBN: 978-1-78264-172-8 | e-ISBN: 978-1-78264-180-3